Using Observations in Small-Scale Research

A BEGINNER'S GUIDE

Mary Simpson
and
Jennifer Tuson

The Scottish Council for Research in Education

SCRE Publication 130

Practitioner MiniPaper 16

First published 1995

Series editors: Wynne Harlen
                   Rosemary Wake

THE SCRE 'USING RESEARCH' GUIDES

Lewis, Ian & Munn, Pamela (1987) *So You Want to Do Research! A guide for teachers on how to formulate research questions.* Practitioner Minipaper 2.

Munn, Pamela & Drever, Eric (1990) Revised edition 1995. *Using Questionnaires in Small-Scale Research: a teacher's guide.* Practitioner Minipaper 6.

Drever, Eric (1995) *Using Semi-Structured Interviews in Small-Scale Research: a teacher's guide.* Practitioner Minipaper 15.

Simpson, Mary & Tuson, Jennifer (1995) *Using Observations in Small-Scale Research: a beginner's guide.* Practitioner Minipaper 16.

ISBN 1 86003 012 2

© The Scottish Council for Research in Education 1995

The views expressed are those of the authors and are not necessarily those of the Scottish Council for Research in Education.

Printed and bound for the Scottish Council for Research in Education, 15 St John Street, Edinburgh EH8 8JR by GNP Booth, Glasgow.

Cover photograph courtesy of the Scottish Consultative Council on the Curriculum.

Contents

Figures

Acknowledgements

We have written this guide largely on the basis of our own experiences as professional researchers. We would like to thank all the pupils and teachers who have, over many years and in many different research projects, tolerated with patience and good humour, our intrusions as observers in their classrooms.

A Guide to the Guide .....

Increasingly, teachers are being encouraged to use observational strategies for a variety of professional purposes – to assess pupils, to evaluate teaching practices, to collect evidence which can inform developments, support claims or justify proposals for action or change, or to provide data as part of a formal research project. In this guide we introduce teachers, who are well practised informal observers, to some of the techniques which transform informal observation into a recognised procedure for data collection. More detailed accounts of these techniques can be found in the sources listed in the references and the further reading sections.

How is 'observation' different from 'just looking'? In what kinds of studies are observations most useful? Why choose observation as a data gathering technique? In Chapter 1 we introduce the technique of observing, give examples of the variety of investigations for which it can be a useful technique, and consider its advantages and disadvantages as a data gathering tool. We also offer a checklist which will help you to choose the best strategy for your study.

What should you look at? How should you record it? The two main methods of recording observational data are presented in Chapter 2: systematic recording and descriptive and narrative recording. This chapter also covers the use of technological aids such as video and audio recording.

Where do you stand? In Chapter 3 we look at how to plan the management of the observation procedures. How do you decide where to stand? What will be your role and relationships with those you are observing? What might be some of the ethical issues involved?

How can you process your data? The most commonly used methods of analysing data are described in Chapter 4. Through the use of examples, we demonstrate how to manage the processing of both quantitative and qualitative data, and how different analytic approaches may be used to answer different types of research questions.

1

Observation as a
Data-Gathering Technique

"How many times a day does that boy do something in class that really irritates me? What does he do all day? How much time does he spend actually working?"

———————

"I'm trying to get the pupils to think like scientists – to observe, make hypotheses, reflect on ideas and so on – but I don't know if I'm succeeding."

———————

"I've always suspected that whatever the teachers say in this school they must be behaving differently towards the girls in computing – otherwise they wouldn't be so turned off by S3 in comparison with the boys."

———————

"Teachers have a tremendous task to deal with when children first come into school – getting them to understand the rules and culture of the classroom. I don't think anyone yet knows how they actually go about it."

———————

A wide range of questions and concerns such as those above can best be explored by gathering information on what is actually going on in a specific situation. There are a number of techniques for gathering information which would constitute 'research data' about people and their activities. For example, if you wanted to find out how teachers managed groups of pupils in mixed-ability classrooms, you could obtain information in a number of ways:

- **Seeking out** data that already exist from the work of others, which have been published in articles and books.

- **Asking** those involved, either by interviewing a sample of teachers, say from different types of schools or different stages of the primary school, or by sending out a questionnaire and systematically collating the responses.

- **Observing** how a sample of teachers actually proceeded in their classrooms in dealing with the issues which are your focus of interest.

This booklet is about the third method – *observation*. However, even in a small-scale research project in which observation is to be the main method of gathering data, you may find it necessary to use some of the other methods in order to ensure that the information you collect will provide a reliable basis for answering the kinds of questions you are asking and for supporting and justifying the answers you find. — reliability.

How is 'observation' different from 'just looking'?

Most of the information we obtain from our surroundings is obtained by looking. But the eye is part of our brain. To see is to think, to report what we see is to interpret the world from our own personal perspective. So what we see is determined by many individual, subjective factors, in particular our own past experiences in any particular situation and all the relevant conceptual frameworks we have already developed in order to interpret the world. In other words, what we expect to see. So how can looking at events be the basis of a research technique?

The personal experience of just looking must be transformed into a public event by the systematic recording of what we see and by subsequent analysis and interpretation. By thinking through and writing down exactly what information we want to collect, how we are going to collect it and what we think it will demonstrate, we begin to make explicit our underlying assumptions about what is going on. As a result, we open up opportunities for ourselves and others to examine our assumptions, to challenge them and offer alternative viewpoints.

Making things public and open to general scrutiny and discussion is one part of the process of making the 'personal' less subjective. It is also necessary, particularly when observing in your own familiar area of work, to 'make the familiar strange' – that is, to try to detach yourself from your own personal automatic interpretation of what is going on, and to try to see events from different perspectives.

At the end of your investigation you will still not have demonstrated beyond all doubt what exactly is going on, but if you have provided some systematically collected information on what may be going on, and have advanced your own thinking and the thinking of others, then your researches will have succeeded.

When faced with the variety of research techniques available for the collection of information, it may seem difficult to decide which approach would be best. In coming to a decision, it is important to remember that no data collection procedure is perfect. Since each has its own strengths and deficiencies, the trick is to maximise the strengths and minimise the deficiencies of the most relevant technique for your particular purposes.

In coming to a decision to use observation as a data collection procedure, you should consider the following:

- In what kinds of studies are observations most useful?
- Why choose observation as a data gathering technique?
- How can you choose the best strategy for your study?

In what kinds of studies are observations most useful?

Observation can often be difficult and complex, but it is also one of the most versatile ways of gathering information. It can be organised to give quantitative or qualitative data, and can be used in a wide variety of studies. It is essential to select the observational techniques, in other words, the specific ways in which you will observe and record, which are appropriate for your study, and this will be determined by the kind of questions you want to address, the kind of phenomena you will be observing and the context in which you will observe them.

Here are examples of some studies, set up for a variety of purposes – raising awareness, solving a problem, evaluating, measuring and comparing, and trying to understand the world of others – in which different techniques of observation have been used.

The technical details of how the observations were undertaken and how the data were processed will be dealt with later.

Study 1: Observation as 'just looking'

Many professionals find that in the rush of the daily demands of their job they have little time to stop, and just look. The simplest form of gathering data by observation involves just that.

In one study of this type, a teacher identified a concern about children who were not a bother, who did not solicit attention, and she set out to investigate this in a very simple way:

> 'I realised there were some children I always classed as 'good' and 'getting on fine' because they simply didn't stick out in the classroom. So I picked on one girl like that and made a conscious effort to note what she was doing all day. Every ten minutes or so, as often as I remembered, I'd just look round and check. I did that for a whole week.'

Even such an informal use of observation can give useful information. This teacher realised that this child was not in fact 'getting on fine' and she determined to try and change her behaviour towards children of this kind.

> 'It made me more aware of children that I maybe should be spending more time with .... it made me aware that some of the quiet children don't get as much attention from me as they should. If they are not forthcoming, just quiet and friendly, sometimes you don't really notice them that much and it doesn't mean that they don't need it... For example, I have made up my mind I am going to spend more time with Sheena, and I am going to talk with her, to find out how she is getting

on, because I've been assuming she's fine because she smiles at me and keeps out of my way. But I really don't know the last time I had a conversation with her.'

This simple study highlights several key features of observation. Although we are using our eyes all the time, observing to gather specific information requires a conscious act to which we devote time. It is a useful exercise to practise this by stopping your routine on-going activities in the supermarket, in the staffroom, at the parents' evening, in the lounge bar, in the committee, in any normal everyday situation, and undertake the conscious act of observing. For many observation studies this act of standing back, making the familiar activities of a situation into objects which you observe in a detached way – 'making the familiar strange' – is an essential factor for success. Success is measured by the extent to which you see things which you otherwise would not have noticed, or things which surprise you, or things which seem suddenly different in their significance from before.

The next stage of the development of an observational strategy is to make your observations more systematic.

Study 2: Making an observation schedule

In this study a group of teachers worked together in an 'action research' mode to solve a problem. They felt that in order to make progress, they would use observation to assess the size and nature of the problem.

'We felt that in each class in this school there were a number of pupils with behavioural problems. They drained our energies by the amount of attention they needed, but the attention was focused on these behavioural problems rather than on their learning needs. We decided we would each pick two of these children in our class and use a tally sheet to record the incidence of their problem behaviours – distracting others, talking when the teacher was talking – and so on. We also recorded what the learning context was – story time, individual maths, writing etc – so we knew what was going on when the behaviour occurred.'

This group devised their own schedule, determining what should be looked for from their own experiences of the pupils' behaviours. They undertook the recording over short periods, half an hour, while the class was taken, by arrangement, by someone else – a visiting specialist, or the Headteacher. They compared their results and discussed the categories they had first selected, expanding them considerably, and re-using them to identify when the target pupils behaved badly (see Figure 1.1). They then decided that the context of learning was probably a key factor influencing bad behaviour, and decided to do a second round of observations, tallying the incidence of the good classroom behaviours of this group of pupils. They used their data and discussions to plan different kinds of learning experiences which they felt would engage the pupils' interests and serve their needs more effectively than the ones they had currently been using.

In this study the observations were made more systematic and quantitative by the use of tally sheets which the teachers had compiled for themselves. In the next chapter we will look further at observation schedules like this. They have several advantages and

Activity:		
Setting:		
Behaviour	**Tally**	**Comments**
Interrupting others		
Talking while teacher talking		
etc		

Figure 1.1   A teacher-devised schedule

disadvantages. It is possible to get started quite quickly with your observations, but you will almost certainly find that your original categories are not sufficient, or not clear enough. The process of re-thinking through the categories, especially if you are discussing it with colleagues, will greatly enhance your understanding of the events you are trying to observe and categorise. Because you will almost always start simply and develop the schedule to meet your needs, you are less likely to find yourself taking on too much. But take care not to get carried away by adding more and more categories to the schedule. Classroom life is very complex and you may find it increasingly difficult to draw a boundary line round what you think is important, but if your schedule gets too long and complex it will be quite unmanageable. In going through the process of deciding what to leave in the schedule and what to throw out you will be learning the hard way why research (like teaching) is called a discipline!

Study 3: Observing by means of a professional schedule

Some commercially-produced schedules are very complex and difficult even for trained researchers to use with ease, but there is an increasing availability of schedules which are accessible to teachers wishing to do research and you may find one in an article or book which fits exactly what you want, as it stands, or with a minor degree of modification.

A good example of such a schedule is the Science Processes Observation Categories (SPOC) designed by a group of English researchers to obtain information on the incidence in primary classrooms of eight process science skills – observing, interpreting, hypothesising, planning, measuring, recording, raising questions and critically reflecting – and on the conditions under which they occurred (Cavendish *et al*, 1990).

This schedule was designed to be used as a research tool, that is by an observer sitting within the classroom while the normal activities of the teacher are underway. The focus of observations using this schedule is an individual pupil. In the original study six individuals in each class were selected as 'target pupils' and each was observed in rotation for blocks of 16 minutes divided into two-minute intervals. In each two-minute interval the observer recorded whether or not the pre-specified set of behaviours had occurred. The 12 general categories of behaviour covered by this schedule include *Seating of target, Audience/interaction, Non-talk pupil activity, Dialogue involving pupil, Other pupil talk* and *Teacher talk.* All are subdivided into finer grain categories. For example, category 10, *Other pupil talk* is subdivided as follows:

10   OTHER PUPIL TALK

10.1	recall of previous learning	10.5	asking for help
10.2	recap of work done	10.6	organising task
10.3	read out/discuss instruction	10.7	non-task.
10.4	about meaning of words		

When data from the use of such a schedule are processed it allows results of the following type to be reported:

'**Interpreting.**   Very little discussion of interpretations was observed. The teacher's involvement in those discussions which did occur was prominent.

Hypothesizing.   Hypothesizing occurred in less than one in ten of the observations, but again the teacher was prominent where it was observed.

Planning.   More than three quarters of the children engaged in discussion of planning at some time, and this was observed in 30 per cent of the two-minute intervals. Teacher involvement was relatively great. There were no consistent differences between ages or achievement bands.

Measuring.   Approximately 10 per cent of the observed intervals included some discussion of measuring. Teacher involvement did not feature highly in these discussions.'

Cavendish *et al* (1990)

A schedule such as this may be used by teachers who wish to judge the effectiveness of a particular teaching strategy, for example one which aims to promote a particular type of behaviour in pupils.

Using a 'before and after' measure of the frequency of the desired behaviour would allow some judgement to be made on the success of the strategy.

A different way of looking at events, behaviours, or interactions in classrooms is by means of a rating scale. These scales are based on the same principle as the 'scores' given to skaters for their technical expertise and their artistic flair. They are based on the assumption that you can rate the qualities or characteristics of different features of the situation you are observing.

For example, a scale devised for rating the qualities of the 'pre-five environment' (McCail, 1991) deals with ten characteristics, including *informal use of language, staff roles, investigations displays and areas*, and *community*. The rating scale for *staff roles* is shown below.

	INADEQUATE 1 2	MINIMAL 3 4	GOOD 5 6	EXCELLENT 7
Staff Roles	Adults have little interaction with the children in their care to further the children's exploration	Adults seek to provide, ad hoc, for the children's need to explore the world around them.	Adults plan the programme with the needs of individual children in mind, talk to the children about the children's discoveries and encourage child-child discussion and role play.	As 5. Also adults work with individual children in whatever way is judged to be most appropriate, guiding them, supplying information, questioning them, directing to picture books or other sources of information, facilitating their dramatic or role play or joining in with their explorations.

Figure 1.2 Pre-five environment quality rating scale

Many sets of performance indicators take the form of rating scales, in which the points on the scale are attached to descriptions of the quality being judged. Note, however, that the ratings on different categories cannot be added to give one overall score.

Sources of information on different schedules will be given as we deal with each type. If you plan to use a ready-made schedule as part of a research investigation you must read carefully all the instructions associated with the schedule chosen, especially with reference to how the categories have been defined. For SPOC for example, categories of behaviour such as *waiting for teacher* or *planning* are defined and examples are given. It is also important to try out the schedule from beginning to end, ie right through to the processing of the data in order to gauge its feasibility, bearing in mind the resources you have at your disposal, particularly your available time. At one stage a SPOC researcher noted of their procedures: 'This produced a total of over 4000 observations of children while they were engaged in science in the project classrooms'. It seems always to be the case that professionally designed schedules produce an awful lot of data!

You will also find it necessary to *practise* using a schedule designed for detailed observations. Watching, categorising, coding and recording in a fast-moving situation can be very demanding, and you may find your first couple of attempts at using a schedule as nerve-wracking as your first attempts at driving a car. Have faith, and you will find that practice improves matters. If it does not, you are over-coding for the situation, and need to look again at whether the schedule should be cut down for your particular purposes.

Study 4: Adapting a schedule to suit your needs
If you cannot find a professionally produced schedule which fits your intended study, or if you find one which is too complex for you to use while you are acting as a teacher as well as a researcher, an option is to adapt an existing schedule. This can best be done either by fine-tuning some parts of the schedule to suit your purpose, or by using a small part of the schedule as a basis for further development.

For example, in one of our research projects, we wished to use the schedule DePICT-3 (Anderson, 1984) which allowed us to monitor six general categories of teacher activities: *orienting, assessing, correcting, maintaining, instructing* and *disciplining,* along with the format and purpose of the segment of the lesson being observed. While we were happy with some of the fine detail of the behaviours included in each category, we felt it necessary for our purposes to include additional sub-categories. For example, in the category *instructing* which included such behaviours as *explains key elements* and *repeats important points,* we felt it necessary to add some additional elements such as *answers own questions, answers pupils' questions,* and *asks questions about pupils' ideas.*

It is important to remember, however, that professionally produced schedules are usually detailed and therefore demanding to use. As a rule of thumb – however much you add to any part of the schedule, be sure to remove an equal amount from elsewhere.

Although the science process observation schedule (SPOC) was developed for research purposes, it was also intended to be a resource for teachers who wished to use parts of it to develop their own observing techniques. Accounts of how some teachers did this can be found in Cavendish *et al* (1990). Other professionally devised schedules which are too complex for general use, such as that of Galton and Patrick (1990) which uses categories dealing with the whole scope of the primary curriculum, can be used in the same way – as a detailed breakdown of categories of classroom interactions and events from which you can select the particular areas of interest in your study.

Study 5: Observing without a schedule

In the studies referred to above, the observers had a fairly clear idea when they started what exactly they wanted to look at. But in some studies the researcher starts from a quite explicit position of uncertainty. If you set out your categories beforehand, you have already decided what the situation is all about, how to chop it up into small categories, what is important and what is unimportant, and you are setting out in some way to quantify the pre-selected activities or processes. A contrasting approach is to view social

PTO

interactions as a series of complex encounters in which personal meanings, individual perspectives, and dynamic interactions are the key factors. This 'naturalistic' or 'ethnographic' approach to research is based on anthropological strategies in which individuals and groups are studied in their social settings. The aim in these studies is to gain further understanding and insights into how different people perceive and interpret events, how they behave in specific contexts, and how they interact with others.

Observation is a key technique in this style of research. The observer approaches the situation to be observed with as open a mind as possible as to what is going on. In the process of discovering the meaning of what has been observed, some tentative categories may be proposed which are tested out as the study proceeds, either by checking these with those observed, or by further observations. Delamont (1992) and Woods (1986) give lively and interesting accounts of the use of this type of research in educational and other settings.

The questions addressed by the use of this technique are directed towards the understanding of human interactions and experiences in particular complex settings. For example:

- How are decisions communicated within a school? Who communicates with whom? What affects the 'status' of the messages?

- How are teachers inducted into the ethos and value culture of a school? Who communicates formal, overt messages about 'proper' values? What informal messages are communicated in the staffroom or by the way in which classrooms are set out?

Here is an account of how one study began.

'My son hated the first two or three years of his secondary school. He came home rebellious and tearful from school claiming he'd been picked on, that the teachers weren't being fair. He wasn't a bad boy or a lazy one – but his teachers – my fellow professionals – couldn't all have been as bad as he claimed! It was a dreadful time. I just couldn't understand what was going on – and I'm an experienced teacher! Then suddenly in fourth year everything settled down. When I got the opportunity to do a research project I took the chance to investigate the phenomenon of 'difficult children'. I just wanted to look at what was going on in their school lives – not the real 'hard mob', the usual gang of delinquents, but the loners, the misfits, the irritants – for reasons no one can quite articulate. I just wanted to try and understand what might be going on.'

Because this researcher did not bring pre-conceived ideas to her investigation, and because she wanted to move towards an understanding of a complex set of interactions, it would have been inappropriate to begin with a pre-structured schedule on to which she would have to fit what she observed. In this type of study it is necessary to begin by simply taking notes – 'field notes' – in the observation setting, and to evolve a set of categorisations for the behaviours or interactions recorded as the study proceeds.

Study 6: Observing by 'being there'

In a study such as number 5 above, it would be possible to conduct the observations by arranging to sit in classrooms or staffrooms with a note-pad and pencil and to take notes on what you see going on, and to supplement the observation notes by talking with others in a formal or informal way about their perceptions of the events you have been watching.

However, it is possible to go even further in attempting to understand the perceptions and actions of others by actually entering fully into their world and taking an active part in their activities and experiences. There have been some famous studies of this type from professional worlds other than that of education – for example, Goffman (1961) arranged to be admitted into a mental hospital to discover from the inside what it was actually like to be a 'mental patient'. Within education it is possible to do a study such as that by Pollard (1985) who, inspired by his introduction to research strategies during his MEd experiences, decided to carry his research activities into his professional setting when he was appointed to a teaching post in a secondary school. This participant method of research is distinct from merely doing research in a professional setting, as it requires the researcher not only to be engaged fully with the people and context which is being researched, but, at the same time, to be detached enough from this engagement to be analytical about his or her own feelings, perceptions and actions within that setting. The researcher in this mode of research thus adopts a dual role, and must commute between being involved and being detached.

Pollard reports that the advantage of being professionally involved was that:

> 'it led to the accumulation of knowledge and awareness which, although often hard to verbalize, was a great asset in analysis and in 'filling in' accounts and in establishing relationships. Another way of putting this would be to say that through my participation I learned 'the code' with all its nuances and subtlety. After all, I was myself 'coping with deviance' within the very same institution and within very similar patterns of constraint and resource as the teachers whom I studied.'

According to Pollard, he acquired knowledge and understanding which would not have come about in any other way. In addition, his involvement:

> ' ... continually renewed my 'credit' with the staff. I was not simply in the role of 'taking' from the school with an air of detached ivory-tower research authority, I was also 'giving to' and of course 'needing' the school, which provided a far more natural balance of rights and obligation on which to build a relationship of trust than a pure observer role could have done. I think this fact is reflected quite regularly in the quality and frankness of the data which I was able to collect. There were, however, considerable technical difficulties regarding my researcher role.'

The major difficulties centred on finding time out from teaching activities to record and process his data, and on how to share, discuss and negotiate the final form of the report of his findings with his colleagues. Participant observation is the most subtly intrusive of all the styles of observing, since involvement gains the researcher access to the normally unseen heart of professionals' activities, and people tend to forget that one of their colleagues has an additional role:

> 'After a period in which the staff were conscious that I was 'doing my research', it appeared to be largely forgotten or to be assumed that, because I spent a lot of time talking to children, I was not investigating elsewhere. I did nothing to dispel this assumption.'

As we will discuss later, this can present the researcher with quite significant ethical dilemmas, particularly when it comes to reporting, and, as Pollard suggests, one of the crucial factors in determining whether you will be successful in pursuing this type of research is your personality, and style of thinking and acting (Pollard 1985, pp230-232).

Although most research of this kind has been undertaken in adult work settings, they have also been done by adults trying to discover what the world is like from the child's perspective. Clearly this can cause quite significant logistical problems!

> 'Two four-year-old girls (Betty and Jenny) and adult researcher (Bill) in a nursery school:

Betty:	You can't play with us!
Bill:	Why?
Betty:	'cause you're too big.
Bill:	I'll sit down. *(Sits down)*
Jenny:	You're still too big.
Betty:	Yeah, you're 'Big Bill'!
Bill:	Can I just watch?
Jenny:	OK, but don't touch nuthin!
Betty:	You just watch, OK?
Bill:	OK.
Jenny:	OK, Big Bill?
Bill:	OK.

(Later Big Bill got to play)'

Corsaro (1981)

Why choose observation as a data-gathering technique?

For many experienced researchers, observation is the most satis-fying technique to use in investigations since it brings forth the *'sweetest'* of data:

> 'Actually observing life in educational institutions is my fa-vourite kind of data-collection. A pile of documents, a well-written book, or a co-operative interviewee may excite others, but I would always prefer to sit and watch something. The data gathered by watching and listening over weeks, even months, are for me the sweetest jams and the most aromatic oils and spices.'

> Delamont (1992)

As professional researchers, we know exactly what she means. But to be more prosaic, what are its key strengths and weaknesses?

Strengths

- *Observation can give direct access to social interactions*
  The major strength of observing is the direct access which it gives you to the events or interactions which are the focus of your research. The records you make will, as a consequence, be more detailed and more direct than data from any other source. Would you be able to get the same information simply by ask-ing people what they do? Almost certainly the answer is 'no'. Very often people do not tell an interviewer all that is relevant to the situation. This may be because they deliberately choose not to, perhaps because they feel that it would be improper, impolite or insensitive to do so. Or it may be that they simply don't think to mention something, and because the interviewer does not have enough information to enquire further, impor-tant factors are overlooked. But it is also the case that many events occur in the life of a social group so regularly that they are never commented on, or questioned, by the participants. Individuals may never have become aware of them in a con-scious fashion, and are therefore unable to talk about them in an open and articulate way.

• *Observation can give permanent and systematic records of social interactions*

There are a number of ways in which observations may be re-corded – by means of field notes, detailed records, rating scales, structured observation schedules or videotape. Whatever type of record is made, it offers a permanent account of a transient situation, an account which can be used in a variety of ways at a later date. Some records offer rich detailed descriptions of class-room life, others offer accounts in terms of strictly defined cat-egories. When these are derived from the careful use of profes-sionally designed schedules, they can be used to compare data collected in the same way at different times and in different set-tings in other studies.

• *Observation can enrich and supplement data gathered by other techniques*

Even if in your study the main method of collecting informa-tion is by interviews or questionnaires, the addition of data gath-ered by observation can greatly enrich and enhance your data base. Any tool for data-gathering provides only one picture of the social world, and matches and mismatches between data gathered by different techniques help to enrich understanding of what is going on. For example, a teacher in an interview may outline for you her policy for dealing in an identical way with boys and girls. How would you seek to interpret this, set along-side observation data which indicate that she asks questions of boys twice as often as of girls, and reprimands girls twice as frequently?

• *Observation techniques are extremely varied*

The main feature of observation, however, is its extreme flex-ibility. There is almost no research strategy to which data col-lection by observation cannot contribute:

- **It can be applied through a wide range of techniques,** for example, by simply looking, as in Study 1; by looking sys-tematically for specific categories of events, as in Studies 2, 3 and 4; and by looking at a social situation and generating categories to explain complex interactions, as in Studies 5 and 6.

- **It can yield very different types of data,** such as immediate, additional information on everyday situations, as, for ex-

ample, in Study 1; detailed, structured, systematic information, as in Study 2; reliable, quantitative data, as in Studies
3 and 4; and rich, complex, detailed accounts of social interactions, as in Studies 5 and 6.

- *It can demand a variety of research skills,* for example, simply looking, as in Study 1; sustained concentration, categorisation and recording, as in Studies 2, 3 and 4; detached,
  non-judgmental, open-minded, sustained attention, as in
  Study 5; sophisticated negotiation of conflicting personal
  and professional roles, as in Study 6.

- *It can be applied in a variety of contexts* – your own classroom; other people's classrooms; communal social areas:
  staffrooms, corridors, dining-hall, playgrounds, playing
  fields, field-centres etc.

- *It can be used to address a variety of types of research questions,* for example: What is going on here? How often does
  X happen? How do these people interact? What seems to
  affect the incidence of X? Are these people actually doing
  what they say they're doing? What makes these events happen the way they do? Am I being successful in what I am
  trying to change?

Weaknesses

If observation as a technique is so useful, why is it not used more
often in research? Generally speaking, it has two main weaknesses:
its high demand on time, effort and resources; and its susceptibility to observer bias. You need to take steps, while planning your
study, to take account of these two weaknesses.

In order not to take on more than you can handle, you should
pilot your observation procedures so that you can make a fair es-
timate at the outset of how long the data collection and processing
might take, then plan your study within the limits of your resources. For further guidance on data processing see Chapter 4.

The second weakness – its susceptibility to bias, which occurs
either because the observer records what he or she thought occurred rather than what actually did take place, or because of the
observer's lack of attention to significant events, is a little more
difficult to deal with. You should therefore try to set out some of

the underlying assumptions about classrooms which you bring to your study and discuss these with teaching colleagues, researchers or people outside the profession. Such discussions will help to remind you of the different ways in which things might be viewed and so reduce bias in your approach. For example, our amendments to the DePict-3 schedule which we mention on page 11, reflected our views of what were key features of an instructional setting. We felt it was important to know the extent to which the teacher, in responding to questions, was answering questions which he/she had raised, or whether the answers were to questions raised by the pupils. This concern follows our commitment to a particular model of instruction which may not be shared by all. In every investigative task where you must limit what you can measure or record, choices must be made which reflect value judgements about what you consider to be important and what you do not. You need to be quite clear in your mind that you can defend your choices and that you have given alternative choices proper consideration.

You should also try to check your interpretation of your observations with that of others who were present, for example, the teacher whose class you were observing, and reflect on the implications of the differences between your account of events and that of others. A good illustration of how to enrich and validate observation data by follow-up interviews is provided in a study by McAlpine *et al* (1988), in which student teachers observed a lesson and noted key events as they occurred. The teacher was questioned as soon as possible after the lesson as to how he/she viewed these events and why specific decisions were taken.

However, the type of questioning used is important. Student teachers who adopted a closed, confirmatory style of questioning in which they sought to confirm their own hypotheses, obtained little in the way of information.

Student A: 'Did you move Linda because she was talking?'
Teacher: 'Yes.'

Students who adopted an open, exploratory style of questioning and suspended their own ideas about what had happened were rewarded with rich additional information necessary for understanding the complex factors associated with what might have appeared to the observer to be a simple situation.

Student B: 'I saw you move Linda. Why was that?'

Teacher: 'Well, you probably saw I had a word with her earlier; twice in fact. The first time I asked if she was having trouble with the work, the second time I warned her I'd move her if she didn't stop talking. You can't move someone every time they talk; if you do, you'll alienate them and they'll always be on your back. You've got to be seen to be fair, give them a chance to tell you if there's a problem. But in the end, you're in charge and can decide enough's enough. If you move them though, you can't just ignore them after that. I know some teachers do and say: "Thank goodness, I'll get on with the rest of the class". I keep giving them attention; if you don't, you lose them for ever.'

How can you choose the best strategy for the study?

We have indicated a variety of ways in which observation can contribute to research studies. The checklist which follows should help you focus on the key aspects of your studies and reach decisions on the kind of observation techniques which will be appropriate.

a) The specific focus of your study

What is it you want to learn more about – teachers' socialisation, mechanisms of communication, children's learning experiences, the effects of the physical environment, play activities?

b) The specific research questions you want to address

Are you trying to describe or understand some situation? Are you trying to quantify the occurrence of certain events? Do you want to compare the incidence of specific types of events in different classrooms?

c) *The focus of your observations*

Who or what are you going to look at or listen to – children's behaviour, children's talk, teachers' activities, social exchanges, instructional exchanges?

d) *Recording your observations*

Are you going to use a recording schedule? Will you make it up yourself or will you use one already developed? Are you going to use a note-pad, a tape recorder, a video recorder?

e) *Where you are going to observe*

Is the setting to be in your own workspace, or in the workspace of other people – the classrooms of others, the staffroom, or playground? How are you going to arrange for this without causing disruption, distortion of events or offence?

f) *The problems you might encounter*

Observing other people is potentially a confrontational and intrusive activity. There are a number of problems which you might encounter. What actions can you take to anticipate and minimise the effects of your activities?

g) *The supplementary information which might be necessary*

Your observational data alone may not be sufficient to support your interpretations of events. Do you also need to conduct interviews, or compare your findings with evidence in documents? What additional sources of evidence might be used to support your claims?

h) *The processing of your data*

Will you be gathering quantitative or qualitative data? What data processing techniques will be appropriate?

Once you have decided on the specific focus of your study and the research questions you wish to answer, you will find Chapter 2 will give you some assistance in considering (c) and (d) and in Chapter 3 we'll deal with the issues associated with areas (e), (f) and (g). The procedures for processing data collected by observation are covered in Chapter 4.

2

Selecting What to Observe and How to Record Your Data

Once you have decided on the exact purpose of your study and the questions to which you want to find answers, you should be close to a decision on exactly who and what you are going to observe, how many people or events you need to observe and what observation and recording techniques are appropriate. In this chapter we deal in turn with these three aspects of planning an observational strategy. However, there is a fourth key aspect which you must also bear in mind when you are planning your study – how your data can be analysed. It's extremely frustrating and disappointing to reach the data analysis stage and find that the research design or data collection procedures don't allow you to analyse the data in such a way that you can answer the research questions.

Who or what should you look at?
Our social lives are extremely complex and you should select with care what to look at, in order to give the most useful and informative data for your study. In planning your investigations it is important to be aware of the complexities of social situations so that you can focus on those aspects which are important as far as the key questions of the study are concerned. One of the most difficult decisions is choosing exactly who or what you are going to select as the observational focus of your study, and putting strict boundaries around it so that your study is kept manageable in terms of scale.

Before starting the agony of taking that decision, indulge once again in 'just looking' at some everyday social situations – in the staffroom, the supermarket, the railway station, the bus queue, the canteen – and consider in an objective way what you see. This exercise should give you experience of the wide range of factors which might be selected for observation and highlight the need for you to identify carefully those few which will be most useful in giving answers to your specific research questions.

Try to identify the key social places
Any area where people meet and interact is likely to have different 'social places'. In the staffroom, for example, there may be a place by the door, extending into the corridor, where people encounter each other accidentally, try deliberately to avoid each other, or try actively to encounter each other. There may be a place such as the coffee queue where they really cannot choose who they stand next to and where, consequently, different kinds of social interactions take place.

Then there will be the seating area – how is that space set out? What effects may that have on social life? Could it have been arranged purposefully to encourage certain social groupings? Or to discourage certain encounters? How do pupils set up and use social areas in the playground? Are there places where only boys go, or which are exclusive to certain age groups, or certain 'gangs'? What effect does the presence of a teacher have? Do adults have their own particular places in the playground?

Try to identify the significant objects
Classrooms were once set out with rows of desks, the larger, teacher's one set high at the front. Religious texts would be on the walls, a round globe of the world in the corner, the blackboard, pointer and strap conveniently to hand. Looking at the objects in a social area can tell you much about what kinds of activities and interactions go on there. If you visit an old folk's home which by its decor and furniture resembles a five-star hotel, will you interpret the information given by staff differently from that received in a shoddy, run-down setting? Look at the characteristics of the objects in a classroom, staffroom, gym, dining-room, supermarket, church, and think of the messages they give you. Will these mes-

sages be the same for all the people who come into the setting and use it socially? What effects might these messages be having on the behaviour observed there?

Try to look in detail at all the activities '

What kind of activities are taking place? Descriptions of activities can vary in their degree of generality and in the extent to which the observer relies on inference in categorising the purpose of the activity. For example, observing at a committee meeting, you will see the general activity of 'conducting business'. You could describe the component behaviours as follows: the distribution of paper, taking minutes, discussing items, recording decisions. These are the activities which you directly observe. However, you might wish to categorise the activities according to their function. For example, scoring points, gaining status, moving the meeting forward, taking advantage, pulling rank, provoking confrontation, etc.

This level of categorisation goes beyond observation, since it clearly requires a high degree of interpretation and inference on the part of the observer, but it is perhaps a more interesting and informative way of describing 'what is really going on'. Although for many schedules this kind of categorisation is the first stage of data analysis rather than data gathering, on some schedules observable events have been pre-categorised by function, for example in the DePICT-3 schedule (see page 39).

However, the higher the degree of inference in a research study, the more danger there is of misinterpretation and the more important it becomes to check out your categorisations by using different kinds of data collection, for example by interviewing some of the people involved to check out what they perceived and experienced in the situation. This does not mean, of course, that if their view disagrees with yours, that your interpretation is wrong, but in a research context, more is needed than simply your opinion against theirs. You need to provide a sound argument, backed up by supplementary data, for example from documents, from descriptions of similar events or from interviews, to substantiate your case. We deal with this in greater detail on page 66.

What might be identified as the significant events?

Events or 'critical incidents' are sequences of activities which are selected for particular attention by the observer and which can be identified by natural boundaries, for example by a teacher initiating a certain sequence of activities by making an announcement, or by boundaries which are defined by the observer. For example, you may wish to select particular kinds of 'discipline events' or 'learning events' as a focus for your observation. The former might be any sequence of activities which is initiated by an act of aggression and which results in a child being disciplined by a teacher; the latter could comprise the allocation of a mathematical task to a child, the child's completion of it, and the teacher's response. Selecting 'the unit' of behaviour, interactions or events is a very important factor in determining the quality of your research and whether the data you gather can begin to answer your research questions.

Who might be identified as the key actors?

While the focus of your investigation may be a 'what' – what is said, what is done, what is achieved – all of these are mediated through the people who engage in the activities you are watching. In your practice observation you can consider a whole range of questions which vary in the degree of inference which you have to make in order to answer the questions. Who are the actors in this scene? What is their role? Who does what? Who do they interact with? How do they interact differently with each other? What are their different goals? How do they achieve their different goals? What feelings might they be having? How do they communicate these feelings to others? What do they say to each other? What might these communications mean?

How you describe people and what they are doing depends very much on the conceptual understandings or frameworks you bring to the study and use in the interpretation of the data. Desmond Morris was trained as a zoologist, and introduced the idea of 'people watching' as an extension of the zoologists' strategy of watching animals in zoos (Morris, 1977). The novelist Fay Weldon, on the other hand, is concerned with the complex and subtle interactions of personal relationships. When she watches and listens to a family at breakfast, she interprets the activities and exchanges in terms of the deep, dangerous hidden dynamics of family life (Weldon, 1976). As you plan your study you should try to become aware of the conceptual frameworks you are using to inform your study, and to question whether there might be other more useful ways of looking at things. You will find useful information on this aspect of research in *Conceptualising Classrooms*, Chapter 2 in Anderson and Burns (1989).

The sample size

Quite often, the main concern of beginner researchers relates to sample size – 'Is it *big* enough?' Unfortunately, because gathering and processing observation data are labour-intensive activities, the sample size in any such study is usually quite small. However, a small sample does not necessarily make the research unsound. When the sample size is small, it is the nature and scope of the claims made which may need to be adjusted, not the size of the sample. For example, the following claim would be appropriate to stand up as the valid outcome of an observational study:

> 'My research shows that secondary teachers in Scotland are very effective, because they use a mixture of traditional and progressive methods.'

A more appropriate outcome would be as follows:

> 'My research shows how a group of seven Religious Education teachers, selected to show a range of years in post, used a variety of teaching styles. The extent to which they achieved the key aims set out in the national certificate course is discussed, and how their idiosyncratic use of discussion appeared to be related to their perceptions of the purpose of teaching RE in their schools.'

Clearly, such a study is small-scale, but there is nevertheless a great deal of substance to it. Studies like these typically use observational methods, and they do not aim to collect representative data or to claim that their findings are widely generalisable. Rather, their aim is to explore the variety and range of views, practices, beliefs etc associated with some aspect of professional life. The sample will be chosen, therefore, to be appropriate for the purposes of the study, rather than randomly. However, there may well be some situations in which it **is** appropriate to sample randomly, even when your sample is small, for example selecting pupils to be observed in a classroom. This may require nothing more than simply selecting names from a hat, but if you require anything more complex than a random sample, for example if you wish to have a representative proportion of boys and girls, consult a text for the appropriate sampling procedures (eg Cohen and Manion, 1994).

Ways of recording observation data

[All observation strategies can be described in terms of two basic characteristics – what is to be observed, and how it is to be recorded – and they can vary very much in terms of these two features.\As we have already indicated in Chapter 1, some strategies allow the observer a great deal of freedom to decide what is going to be observed during an observation session. The outcome of such a session would be relatively unstructured notes on what has been noticed. Other strategies are based on a highly structured schedule in which all the categories of behaviour which are of interest are pre-specified on the recording sheet, and the rules for classifying behaviour into the different categories and timing the observations are pre-determined and applied by all researchers using the schedule. Whichever strategy you use, you may also find that additional records are useful – for example, a record sheet which you or the teacher completes which puts the observed activities into context in terms of the day's timetable, the current topic or theme, the resources used and the basis on which the pupils are grouped. A diagrammatic classroom plan can also be invaluable in helping you to keep track of pupils' movements, or indeed the distribution of teacher attention at different stations etc.

\Generally speaking, recording systems can be divided into three types, systematic recording (using fixed schedules), descrip-

tive recording (using descriptive and narrative records) and technological recording (using cameras, video or audio tapes). ⎰

Systematic recording

This is used in what is described as *structured observation* in which
the observer assigns what is observed into previously specified or
defined categories, and records it on a prepared schedule according to agreed procedures. These procedures are used to gather data
which can be treated quantitatively, summarised in numerical
form, and related to other data using simple statistical techniques.
The purpose of studies which use these types of schedule is to
quantify the incidence of particular classroom events, to seek relationships which can be tested by statistical methods and which
may be generalised to hold across similar cases. If the schedule
has been used by an observer applying the correct procedures for
its use the observations should be unaffected by personal biases
and all observers should arrive at roughly similar descriptions of
the same events. Here we can deal only with examples of the most
commonly used types of schedules. For a fuller account of these
procedures you should consult Croll (1986).

What should be the 'unit' observed?

Most structured observation schedules require observers to focus
on one 'unit' only. In classrooms the focus would normally be the
teacher, or an individual student, or a group of interacting pupils.
A selection must also be made, determined by the purpose of the
research, of particular aspects of their behaviour to be recorded.
For example, if the purpose of the study is to examine some aspect
of teachers' activities in the classroom – what they say, what they
do, or how they allocate their time etc – the focus will clearly be on
the teacher and the relevant behaviour. If the purpose is to examine specific activities of the pupils, the focus will either be selected
individuals or pupils in an interacting group, and again it would
be restricted to the particular behaviour of interest in your study.

Given the complexity of interactions in the classroom, it may
seem inappropriate to narrow the focus too much, but it is extremely difficult for one observer to record systematically a wide

range of features in the classroom, and the research questions should be narrowed so that the data gathering has a manageable focus. This would normally mean that the schedule of categories of people and behaviour to be looked at can be summarised on one sheet of paper, since you are likely to miss seeing things if you are distracted by shuffling paper. For further information on 'units of analysis', see Burstein (1987).

Event recording systems

The simplest systematic recording system can be devised as was indicated in Study 2, in which events are recorded as they occur on a schedule in which a list of behaviours is set out and the observer simply tallies how often the behaviour takes place over a given time period. For example, the tally sheet shown below might be used to count the instances of disruptive or learning-avoidance behaviour of an individual child.

John Smith	Date: 20/2 Time: 10.05 Duration: 30 mins Subject: Maths	Date: 22/2 Time: 11.35 Duration: 30 mins Subject: Language	Date: 24/2 Time: 3.00 Duration: 30 mins Subject: Music	etc
Twisting or clenching hands	HHH HHH HHH III	HHH HHH HHH HHH III		
Rocking body/head	HHH III	HHH HHH I	I	
Distracting neighbours	HHH HHH III	HHH III		
Making nonsense sounds: humming, talking to self	III	HHH III		
Thumb-sucking	HHH II	III	II	

Figure 2.1 A tally system of recording

Such a tally system is very simple, but might well be subjected to considerable refinements if it is repeatedly used and the outcomes shared and discussed with others. Nevertheless, such a simple schedule can be sufficient for specific purposes. For example, a record such as the one above might tell you that in any given period a particular child picked his nose ten times, fell off his seat eight times, interrupted other children 27 times and was rebuffed by other children 15 times; that he was smiled at by the teacher five times and reprimanded 18 times, and that the pattern was totally different when the music specialist took the class. Such information might form a basis for identifying patterns of learning or behavioural difficulties associated with different contexts and planning a programme to improve matters.

A similar schedule could be constructed to look at teachers' activities, perhaps in a co-operative observation study between two teachers. You might start off with quite general activities in the list of behaviours, for example *'keeping discipline', 'asking questions', 'responding to pupils' queries'* etc. But, depending on the purpose of the exercise, you might find these behaviours too general, and decide that a more detailed breakdown is necessary. At this stage you will probably find it necessary to select which kinds of activities you are really interested in, otherwise the schedule becomes unmanageable. Is the focus to be the teacher's relationships with specific children, or more general features of discipline and child management, or the management of the curriculum, or particular kinds of learning activities? Itemising specific observable elements for any one of these general areas is likely to produce a fairly extensive list, but for manageability it is essential that you have the full list of categories all on one page. However, through the process of refinement and reduction you will almost certainly learn a considerable amount about how you and your colleagues think about your classroom practices and behaviours, and the relevance of this for the interpretation of your data.

A tally schedule such as the one above is a simple event-recording instrument, ie its purpose is to make a frequency count of particular events. How does such a data gathering technique work? Imagine you have a camera and you are interested in taking pictures of children when they appear puzzled or surprised. You would not waste film by continually taking pictures, you would be more likely to wait until a child was showing surprise and quickly snap them. At the end of the day you would have a pile of pictures; the order in which they were taken wouldn't matter, because each would simply be a representation of an instance. But you would be able to say – if you were sure you had caught every example – how often the children in the class expressed surprise.

A recording system which is 'event-driven' works in a similar way, ie when certain categories of events occur, they are recorded. The tallies in the boxes above represent the piles of pictures taken of each event in the half-hour recording periods.

But you might want to know more about events associated with the occurrence of the puzzled faces, for example, had they something to do with what the teacher did? In order to link aspects of events you would need a more complex schedule.

To use a more likely example, suppose you wanted to look at the kinds of questions teachers asked of their pupils: whether they were open or closed; whether they were directed more towards boys or girls; whether the tone was different for boys and girls. A schedule to record such events might look like this:

Time						
10.00 am	OBJ	OBJ	CGS	OBS		
.02						
.04	OBJ	CGH	OBJ			
.06	OCS	OCS	OCS			
.08	OBS	OBJ	OBS	OCS	CCH	

Figure 2.2 An event recording schedule

KEY

Question type:	O – open	Target pupils:	B – boy	Tone:	J – jocular
	C – closed		G – girl		H – hectoring
			C – class		S – serious

To use this type of schedule you would need the help of a digital clock or a watch with a second hand so that you could keep track of two-minute time intervals and code the events as they occurred in the appropriate sequence. The time is blocked in two-minute periods for convenience of recording, and to cope with the rate of events as they occur. For infrequent events, the timescales could be longer. This type of schedule essentially yields a tally of complex events and their occurrence over time. If the time of their occurrence was irrelevant, their incidence could be more simply tallied on a sheet on which a box had been provided for every possible pattern. If the monitoring of too many patterns is attempted, the level and rate of decision-taking may place too many demands on the observer, and the schedule – and hence the research questions – might therefore have to be revised.

The kind of information you would collect from the above schedule might be as follows:

"For Mr J's class, over 45 minutes of recording, 87 questions were asked: 74 directed to boys, 13 to girls (NB ratio of boys to girls in class 2:1). Of the questions directed to the boys, 78% were open (50% of these were serious, 45% jocular); of the questions directed towards the girls, 37% were open (25% of these were serious, 10% jocular). 80% of the open, scene setting questions in the early part of the lesson were directed towards boys; such questions directed towards girls were scattered evenly throughout the lesson."

This type of recording is quite demanding because it is almost a continuous record. However, the more infrequent the type of event which is the focus of the record, and the fewer the decisions which have to be made about each event, the more manageable it is. You will need to practise using the schedule in a pilot run so that you can judge the frequency of events and the level of demand of the decision taking. These together will determine how long you can keep up your recording activities. If you find yourself recording only one event each half hour, or 60 per minute, you should reconsider what you are about in order to make the process both worthwhile and manageable.

It is also possible to use a schedule like this to code the beginning and end of events or teaching episodes. You might, for example, wish to record the length of time which teachers and children are engaged in talking. A code similar to that above could be used to indicate the beginning (B) of a teacher (T) talking about the content (C) of a lesson, ie BTC, in contrast with an episode of talk concerned with managing (M) resources or activities, for example BTM. The end (E) of each episode could be similarly coded, for example ETM. Such a record would give you an absolute measure of the time spent on particular activities. Once again, manageability determines that your categories should be broad, or infrequent, or few in number.

One of the distinctions you will come to appreciate as you revise your schedule is the difference between *topographical* and *functional* categories. The list on the tally sheet above is a topographical one – it lists behaviours which you can readily identify as having occurred or not. You could, however, decide that what was important was not simply what behaviours occurred, but their underlying function or purpose. You might decide that *thumb-sucking* and *rocking body/head* were functionally equivalent – different behaviours which served the same purpose, ie they are 'comforting activities'. *Making nonsense sounds* etc and *twisting/clenching hands* might be grouped together as 'displacement activities'; *distracting neighbours* might join *shouting out loudly* as 'attention seeking'.

Clearly if you classify behaviours according to intention or purpose you will be making many assumptions and inferences, but your records will result in a more meaningful description of classroom behaviours. Here is another example from observations of a teacher.

Let us suppose that you see a teacher scanning the class. The next event might be a comment such as, 'I think you've all now more or less finished the note-taking. Can you gather round, please ...' The function of the scan would be inferred to be 'checking progress', a function also served by the teacher asking a question: 'Anyone not finished their note-taking? Hands up!' Both such behaviours, scanning and asking that question, could thus be regarded as functionally equivalent and categorised together as examples of 'checking progress'. In contrast, a class scan accompanied by the comment, "Eyes front! Come on! Pay attention!" could be categorised as 'attention-securing behaviour', as could a sharp hand-clap, or a series of raps on the desk with a pencil.

Whether you select or devise a schedule using topographical or functional categories will depend on the purpose of your research. Although functional categories usually provide more useful information than topographical, they clearly entail more assumptions on the part of the creator of the schedule, and more inferences on the part of the observer. In practice, many schedules are a mixture, with behaviours grouped together by their inferred function.

As soon as you begin to seek agreement with colleagues on the purposes of classroom activities, on how to classify behaviours, and on how to select what is important and what is not, you will be articulating, sharing and seeking agreement on your conceptualisation of the basic nature of classroom relationships. This is an extremely useful and informative exercise and you may well find the process of designing the schedule has been as worthwhile as the product – the schedule itself.

Time-sampling recording systems

If you want to look at a more complex and comprehensive set of events in the classroom you have to use another strategy for recording. The most commonly used schedules which allow more complex categories of events to be looked at in detail are not event-driven but time-driven. Using the previous analogy of taking pictures, the time-driven recorder simply takes a snap picture of the classroom in all its complexity at predetermined time intervals over the observation period. How does this work?

Suppose you took a picture of a primary classroom from the same vantage point every 30 minutes. The pictures would look very different, and you couldn't be sure you had a series of pictures which had caught all the different kinds of events which went on in that classroom. If you took a picture every 0.5 seconds you would end up with a huge pile of pictures, many of them almost identical. What would be the interval between pictures which would allow you to say with confidence, "I have documented a representative sample of views of what this classroom is like"? Once again, the answer really depends on the kind of study you are doing, but the time intervals chosen by professional researchers tend to be in the range 5 seconds to 5 minutes.

In order to find the optimum time-interval, researchers usually trial the use of a number of different time-intervals. For example, comparisons between one- and two-minute interval observations may indicate that the results will be similar whichever time-interval is used. The latter would then be the preferred choice, since it would be less demanding on the observer and would reduce the data-processing required. A longer time-interval might reduce the discrimination power of the instrument – only a trial could determine the optimum interval necessary to secure sound data to answer any specific set of research questions.

The SPOC schedule which we mentioned earlier in Chapter 1 (Study 3) is an example of a time-sampling schedule in which the sample period is two minutes – ie during every interval of two minutes, a record is made of what is going on. An example from this schedule is shown below. Each column of ticks (1 to 6) represents the observations made of the specific behaviours listed in this category in a succession of two-minute intervals.

In this extract, the category of 'non-talk pupil activity' is subdivided into 14 components. The columns 1 to 6 represent two-minute time-sampling intervals.

During each two-minute interval, a series of records (ticks) is made indicating the specified activities in the relevant categories. In the example above, several non-talk pupil activities have been engaged in by the target pupil in each of the two-minute periods. The ticks would have been put in as each behaviour occurred, and once a box had been ticked for these particular activities during that two-minute period (for example, using other materials/equipment) it would not be ticked again during the same interval, however many more times it occurs. This method of recording clearly does not allow you to record how many times an activity occurred in that time in the way that a tally sheet does, but it does tell you that it occurred at least once, how regularly it occurred over the whole observation session, and reveals any pattern of changes in occurrence over time. For example, looking at the distribution of ticks would allow you to see whether certain activities were distributed evenly throughout the lesson, or occurred only at the beginning.

	1	2	3	4	5	6
NON-TALK PUPIL ACTIVITY						
8.1 making observations	√	√	√			
8.2 planning independently						
8.3 using measuring instruments	√	√				
8.4 using other materials/equipment	√	√	√	√		
8.5 collecting, clearing equipment						
8.6 reading book/worksheet etc						
8.7 recording (not copying)	√	√				
8.8 copying from book, worksheet, board				√		
8.9 waiting for teacher		√	√	√		
8.10 waiting for other pupils			√			
8.11 attentive to teacher						
8.12 attentive to other pupils						
8.13 non-attentive to task		√	√	√		
8.14 non classifiable						

Figure 2.3 Coding using SPOC category 8

The kind of information which this system of recording allows you to generate about classrooms has already been indicated on page 8, for example:

'**Recording**: In one out of ten of the observation intervals, children were observed discussing recording. The teacher was involved in those discussions on one-fifth of occasions.'

Category and sign systems of recording

In reading about recording systems you may come across the terms 'category' and 'sign' systems. The earliest observation schedules, which were devised in the 1970s, tended to be category systems in which all the interactions which took place had to be coded under one of the given, discrete categories. For example, the category of *teacher talk* might include the sub-divisions of:

- praising/encouraging
- lecturing
- asking questions
- giving directions
- disciplining
- other/silence

With such a system, *all* instances of *teacher talk* have to be coded in each set time-interval, and have to be fitted into the given categories of classification. The main categories (usually up to ten) are necessarily broad, for example, *teacher talk, pupil talk* and in each there is usually one sub-division (other/silence) which is used to code everything that doesn't fit into the other sub-divisions. The outcome is that in the category of *teacher talk*, the teachers' behaviour is continually monitored, that is to say, something is recorded for every time-interval. But only a coarse-grained picture emerges, there is little fine-grained detail. Such a picture might be all that is required for some aspects of what you wish to record, but it requires you to take decisions continually about how to categorise events which may not be of key interest to your study, and it may not give fine enough detail in those areas which are of particular interest. For these you might prefer a finer-grained analysis, with the key events or behaviours in which you are interested being ticked only if and when they occur.

A combination of these two systems would give you a schedule like the SPOC one, in which some categories are brief and broad, and are coded for each observation period (this is a category system) and in which other categories offer a set of fine sub-divisions, which are coded only if they happen to occur (this is the sign system). In the SPOC schedule the *'seating of target pupil'* category would be ticked without fail for each observation period. The subdivisions in this category allow for all eventualities: *alone; same sex pair; mixed sex pair; same sex group; mixed sex group; whole class.* A similar category system is used for the teacher – whatever the teacher is doing is coded for each observation period in very general terms, for example *monitoring, involved, not present.*

Other parts of the schedule are designed as a sign system so that entries are made only when specific behaviours are observed; for example, the section on dialogue involving the pupil is very detailed, but if the pupil is not engaged in any dialogue in any two-minute period, no record is made in that section. Similarly, if he/she is engaged in dialogue which falls outside the science area of interest of this schedule, that is to say, if it is non-science-related talk, it is simply not recorded. The use of a sign system allows you to operate a fine focus on only the key behaviours which are of interest, and reduces the burden of attending to and deciding about classification of incidents of no interest to your study. You can find more details about these different types of coding in Cavendish *et al* (1990), Chapter 3.

The ORACLE schedule, which also shows the combined use of these two systems of recording, was devised for observation in primary classrooms as part of a major research programme (Galton *et al* 1980). Here, the target pupil's behaviour is coded at regular 25 second intervals. The *target's activity*, his or her *location*, together with the *teacher's activity* and *location* are always coded for each interval. Depending on what the pupil is doing, a set of alternative categories can then be selected for coding, for example, one for the target pupil interacting with the teacher; a different one for his or her interaction with other pupils. These categories have a 'fine-grain' set of sub-divisions – there are 14 for the recording of the target pupil's behaviours. The full details of the ORACLE schedule are set out in the book *Inside the Primary Classroom'* (Galton *et al*, 1980).

The DePICT-3 schedule is of similar construction and a detailed account of the rationale behind its design can be found in Anderson (1984). This schedule has a sample time of 30 seconds and focuses on teachers' activities. The first category, *lesson segment*, is used to record the format (*lecture/demonstration* etc) and purpose (*procedural/instructional*) for each observation interval. It then has six functional categories each with several sub-divisions comprising activities which can be observed. In such a schedule, the first level of analysis has clearly already been done by the pre-categorisation of actions according to their inferred functions. The six categories are as follows:

- orienting: presents objectives
                   communicates high expectation... etc
- correcting: reviews assignments
                   suggests correction... etc
- instructing: explains key elements
                   activates prior learning... etc
- maintaining: provides incentives
                   maintains flow... etc
- assessing: checks assignments
                   assigns practice/homework... etc
- disciplining: issues behavioural warning
                   directs disciplinary action... etc

In a recent study of Scottish secondary classrooms, we used the DePICT-3 schedule in a modified form, having added some sub-divisions to some of the categories and dropping or re-wording others. We also changed the sampling time from 30 seconds to two minutes to match the SPOC schedule which we had also adapted for our particular purposes. These adaptations allowed one observer in the classroom to monitor in detail the teacher's activities while another observed and recorded the activities of a target pupil. As was determined for the SPOC schedule, the two-minute interval afforded an appropriate sampling rate for the behaviours observed and presented the observers with a manageable level of demand with respect to observing, decision-taking and recording.

Published schedules are continually being changed and modified for different purposes. Hargreaves, in Galton and Patrick (1990), describes how the ORACLE schedule was modified for their study in small primary schools, and identifies the constraints which consequently had to be put on comparisons of their data with those from the ORACLE project. One of the adaptations made to the ORACLE schedule by their PRISMS (Curriculum Provision in Small Schools) study was in the sampling time – it was reduced from 25 to five seconds! How can recordings be taken so rapidly? Imagine your recorder photographer employing a rather specialised technique – the one employed when photographing celebrities arriving at shows. The photographer will point the camera at one group and fire off a rapid series of shots. He or she will then pause and turn their attention elsewhere and fire off another rapid series of shots. So, for example, when using the section of the PRISMS schedule to record pupil behaviour, the observer would pause, focus on one of the target children in the class and record the child's behaviour every five seconds. After making ten such recordings and noting the child's task, the observer would pause, and turn to focus on the next target child, and so on until all nine target pupils in the class had been observed. The teacher was observed in a similar fashion at six regular intervals during each lesson. Both the teacher's and the pupils' behaviour were recorded in terms of a set of general categories of *talk, non-interactive behaviour, audience* and *location*.

The full set of sub-divisions for this schedule is set out in Galton and Patrick (1990). These adaptations were made to allow single pupils to be observed fairly intensively for a few hours over the course of the study The researchers wished to have a detailed picture of the activities in which individuals were engaged at a particular time, with further 'snapshots' being taken at intervals throughout the year.

The results are similar in style to those from other studies in which this type of recording has been used, and the use of the schedules in a standardised way allows comparisons to be made.

'When all the observations are put into just three major categories, 71 per cent of observations were task-focused, and this increased to 86 per cent if routine task-supporting jobs, such as sharpening pencils or ruling lines, were included. Only 13 per cent of the observations were coded as off-task or distracted behaviour such as chatting or daydreaming. In the ORACLE study, the equivalent proportions were 64 per cent task work, 17 per cent routine jobs, and 19 per cent distraction. The PRISMS children, then, worked harder.'

Hargreaves (1990)

Clearly, this strategy for recording allows very fine-grain pictures to be taken, in which even pencil-sharpening and day-dreaming can be given a place. Such responsiveness to fine detail can only be sustained in the short, intensive observation strategy we have described above.

As we have indicated, there are several ways in which you can use such schedules. You can read the associated literature and decide to train yourself to use the schedule and its coding system as the designers intended. For the training procedures in the use of the ORACLE schedule, see Appendix 1 in Galton *et al* (1980). If the schedule fits your purposes, you have the advantage of knowing you have collected data using a finely-honed tool, and you can compare your results with the results obtained by others who have used the schedule.

Alternatively, you may decide to adapt the schedule in some way to make it more suitable for what you want to do. However, it would still be extremely useful to read the designer's literature first, since there may be very good reasons why some things should not be changed too much! You may change the schedule by dropping out some of the general categories and/or expanding or changing some of the finer sub-divisions in some of the general categories. You may retain the whole schedule substantially as in the original, but decide that a sampling rate of 25 seconds is unnecessarily fast for your particular requirements, and re-set the time-clock for around two minutes. This would simply mean that your rate of recording and hence the number of samples had dropped. By trying out different rates, you will find out whether the changes in the data gathered will affect the degree to which they allow the research questions to be addressed.

Using a schedule which professionals have designed is like learning to use a complex and sophisticated piece of machinery. It will be very difficult to use until you are familiar with its structure and categories, and you may need to work up slowly to its appropriate sampling rate. But like all precision tools, if it is the right one for the job, it is worth the effort of learning to use it skilfully.

Rating scales

Some schedules are quite different in purpose and structure and allow you to record behaviours or social interactions according to their rating on a scale. For example, a teacher may be rated as harsh or kind; a lesson as dull or interesting; a pupil as aggressive or non-aggressive. Sometimes the points on the scale will simply be designated by numbers:

flexible	1	2	3	4	5	*inflexible*
hostile	1	2	3	4	5	*not hostile*

The problem with such simplicity, however, is obvious – how can an observer be sure that two teachers rated as '3' on the 'flexibility' scale are really 'equal' in this characteristic? And if two observers are contributing to the data, can you be sure their 'scales' are matched? An act which is perceived as 'hostile' by one rater may not be classified as hostile by another.

The answer is to specify as clearly as possible what these ratings mean. In many areas of professional life, for example, pre-service assessment, staff appraisal and school inspection, performance indicators are used which take the form of a rating scale accompanied by the specifications for the ratings to be given. For example, a rating schedule which was developed in Scotland especially for observation in primary school classrooms is the System for Classroom Observation of Teaching Strategies – the SCOTS schedule. In the early chapters of his book, *The Teacher's Craft,* Powell describes how the schedule was developed (Powell, 1985). If you think a rating scale might be appropriate for your purposes, you will find this a useful source of information.

In developing or selecting an appropriate rating scale or, indeed, any schedule, for your own studies, there are three questions to keep in mind:

1. *Do the categories to be rated adequately cover the range of behaviours or features in the area of interest which your observed target group normally exhibit?*

For example, the SCOTS schedule covers ten areas of teaching activities: teaching skills, feedback and individual aid, pupil interest and motivation, development of responsibility, level aimed at, grouping, efficiency of management, authoritarianism and coercion, class control and teacher personality and relationships with pupils. If the last two categories had been missed out, areas considered of high significance by most educators would have been excluded.

2. *Do the set of descriptors for the points on the scale adequately describe the range of possibilities in the aspects which have been selected?*

Part of the SCOTS rating scale for the teachers' relationships with pupils is as shown in Figure 2.4 on the next page.

This sub-category, which is concerned with the rating of the teacher's use of praise and of blame, is designated as the *teacher's approach to the pupils.* If any of the points on the scale had been absent, the full range of possibilities in this category would not have been dealt with.

There are five boxes in which ratings can be made because, for this schedule, it is recommended that five observation periods of a quarter day each should be conducted, with all four quarters of a day being represented at least once. As you can appreciate, a single visit could result in the recording of a teacher on an untypical occasion. The designers of this schedule decided that five observation periods were appropriate.

Negative/Positive Approach Rating Scale	No of observation session				
	1	2	3	4	5
1 Teacher emphasises error and wrongdoing. Praise is almost completely absent; even when pupils produce good work the smallest defect is picked on.					
2 Teacher emphasises error and wrongdoing, and although praise is given it tends to be grudging, half-hearted, or casual.	√			√	
3 There are no strong indications of a positive or a negative approach or both are approximately equal.		√	√		√
4 Teacher tends to praise rather than blame. The general atmosphere is supportive but the use of praise is less systematic than in '5'. (Negative instructions/comments may be converted into positive ones, but less regularly than in '5').					
5 Teacher seeks opportunities to praise good or improved work/conduct and emphasises what has been achieved. Criticism and prohibition are almost completely avoided, positive comments/ instructions being substituted.					
NOTE: Praise that is indiscriminately and cursorily conferred (for example, without even looking at what is praised) should be weighted lightly.					

Figure 2.4 Extract from SCOTS rating scales

3. *Do the specifications accompanying the schedule give observers enough guidance in how to make their judgements, such that two independent observers would rate the same observed activities in the same way?*

The descriptors in the set of ratings as shown above accompanied by additional notes (see Powell, 1985, Chapter 3) assist the users of the schedule to make their judgements without undue subjectivity or bias. Ticks are put in the boxes on each of the five visits, and the final rating is a summary judgement. The main criticism of the use of rating scales is that they can be described as 'high inference', that is, the codings given depend to a considerable extent on the judgement of the individual observer. The design of the schedule, its accompanying notes and the recommendations for its use (for example, the five visits) are strategies for reducing the level of personal bias in the ratings. But as Powell suggests:

> 'It is a primary aim of the SCOTS schedule to allow the observer freedom of *inference within defined limits*. The observer has to be more than an efficient machine recording accurately what occurs: he has to make use of his understanding of what he sees occurring.' (p 17)

So far, we have been describing how to do structured observations using recording instruments which are designed so that, as far as is technically possible, the professional expertise and experience of the observer are excluded, or are applied strictly *'within defined limits'*, once the schedules are in use to collect information.

As we have already indicated in Chapter 1, in our descriptions of Studies 2 to 4, the use of pre-structured schedules allows research questions of particular types to be addressed. The construction, selection or adaptation of the schedule refines researchers' thinking about the precise categories of behaviour or interactions which are of relevance for their studies, and objectivity can be optimised by applying the standard procedures we have described for the use of such schedules. In other types of studies, for example Studies 5 and 6, the starting premise is that much has to be learned about the research setting before the relevant questions can be formulated and a quite different set of techniques needs to be used. We deal now with this particular approach to observation.

Descriptive and narrative recording

Both descriptive and narrative records offer descriptions of classroom events which are considerably less pre-specified in terms of what is selected for attention than those of formally structured records. The distinction between descriptive and narrative records is simply a matter of the degree of initial pre-specification and the scope of what is observed. They have in common the fact that they deal with broad segments of events or processes within naturally occurring time-spans, and they can take account of the time sequences of events and their complex and subtle interactions.

Descriptive records

A descriptive system for recording may have some pre-set categories, but they are much broader and more flexible than those of category systems. Their flexibility allows the observer to consider the context of the behaviours, their sequences, their meanings, and to use naturally occurring events as the starting points and finishing points of recording sequences.

Extracts from descriptive records of pupils dealing with a maths task might look like this:

Observation Pupil Number 1

9.45   *P1 started task. Opens book, writes date. Works intermittently, stops frequently, looking at work of neighbour. When not writing taps pencil rapidly against her lower lip.*

9.55   *Has completed two sums. Incorrect.*

9.57   *Teacher assists; corrects; talks through method; demonstrates in next two sums; departs.*

10.05   *Has completed next two sums. Incorrect. Is looking round to see where the teacher is. Continuous pencil tapping. Avoids teacher's eyes. Tries to read neighbour's work, neighbour objects and leans on her to push her away. Exaggeratedly engrossed in writing as teacher approaches.*

10.17   *Teacher investigates, revises method, talks through and helps P1 complete two more sums.*

10.20   *Teacher departs.*

10.25   *P1 hums, looks round class, surreptitiously observing neighbour. Copies correct answers for next two sums without neighbour being aware.*

        Final result: 10/10.

Observation Pupil Number 2

9.45   *P2 started task. Opens book, writes date, looks round class-*
room. Swinging on chair. Initiates discussions with others
at table on: school photographer's impending visit, owner-
ship of pencils on table, how late he stays up to watch TV.

10.15   *Has completed two sums without much apparent concen-*
tration. Both correct. Still looking round. Intermittently
humming a tune.

10.25   *Continuing to socialise as above. Has been reprimanded*
twice by teacher in last five minutes about his chatting.
No further work done.

10.30   *Teacher announces that they should complete maths exer-*
cise and prepare to tidy up before music. P2 starts sum
number 3.

10.35   *Has completed the 10 sums. All correct.*

Final result: 10/10.

In such a record, a specific segment of classroom life has been selected, ie engagement with a maths task. Multiple aspects of the
behaviours are recorded, and the sequence and continuity of events
are preserved – this cannot be achieved by the use of category
systems. The times noted are linked to the natural events of the
situation, they are not pre-set, fixed time-intervals as are normally
the case with category systems. Descriptive records are usually
made in concentrated time blocks of about 30 minutes, and focus
on some particular aspect of classroom interactions.

Records such as these can be used for a variety of purposes. In
this particular study the information sought by the observer related to the general question: 'How does the target child engage
with this maths task?' and the records were used to formulate
hypotheses about the capabilities and competencies of these pupils in tackling this task, which was doing maths problems involving multiplying by five. These hypotheses were then immediately
tested out by means of further interactive tests with the pupils on
the specific topic of multiplication.

It was hypothesised, for example, that Pupil 2's capabilities were beyond that of the work in which he had been engaged. The researcher immediately selected further, more difficult multiplication tasks for the child to tackle and secured written evidence of his competency in more difficult and advanced work. The hypothesis that the work overestimated the capabilities of Pupil 1 was upheld by the record of the pupil's subsequent discussions with the researcher on her understanding and use of multiplication, and by the outcomes of simple tasks which demonstrated her problems with the concept of multiplication, with hundreds, tens and units, and with making sets of concrete materials.

Descriptive records can be used to record not only what is done (for example, a question is asked) but *how* it is done (for example, sarcastically or cautiously). Because they comprise a detailed, readily understood, sequential record of events, they provide a permanent record which can be re-read and re-analysed by the recorder or by others. In this study of pupils' learning (Simpson *et al*, 1989), the descriptive records were read by two additional researchers who made independent judgements about the classification of the pupils' experiences as reported in the observation records.

In this illustration the observational records were supplemented by material from the pupils' performances on a follow-up task. Descriptive studies may also use video or audio recordings to supplement the immediate observational record. By this means, for example, detailed transcripts of verbal interactions can be analysed in conjunction with notes which detail the non-verbal context with which the conversations were associated. Descriptive systems can be used in this way to apply pre-selected categorisations to events, but the unfolding sequences of processes and interactions are retained, and in contrast to systematic recording with a schedule, the coding is done after the records have been obtained.

Narrative systems or field notes

Narrative systems are used to obtain detailed descriptions of interactions or events without starting from pre-specified categories. The aim of studies in which they are used would be to seek patterns of behaviour in specific situations, to understand specific cases and perhaps to compare the findings across cases. |

| What is observed is selected according to the content focus of the study, but no structure or restriction is put on what is observed, at least in the initial stages. The categories of interest in these records are derived from analysis of the data after the observations, not set out before they take place. The strategy here is to start with fairly general research questions, and to tighten things up gradually as the study proceeds. For example, observations may be planned to address questions such as 'What is school life like for children who show disruptive behaviour?' – 'What particular rules of school life are disruptive children violating?' – 'Do all disruptive children show similar patterns of behaviour?' The data collection technique adopted might be to follow or 'shadow' a sample of individual pupils in this category in one particular school in order to record descriptive accounts of what happens to them in the course of a day, or several days, or even a week of school life. |

The record obtained from this narrative system of recording might look like this:

Class H   1st Period   7.04.91   Science Mr B   Pupil C

9.04   *C comes into the class alone, bunch of girls in front, pair of boys behind – A and J. C is swinging his bag, sweeps it very close to the apparatus on the bench as he goes to his place. (Mr B not noticing?) C goes to second front bench. Takes off anorak with back to Mr B – standing at side of front bench.*

Mr B has spotted C is chewing – while he is announcing about worksheets not having been handed in from last week, is giving repeated pointing gesture to bin, having momentarily fixed C in his gaze. C saunters/slouches up to front, puts gum in bin. (Battle joined very early today. Mr B not in best mood, sentences short, more clipped than usual.)

As C passes Mr B on way back asks, "Please, Sir" if he can have his jotter back from last week, since he hasn't finished his report? Mr B ignores him, carries on talking about

*plan for lesson. Dismissively waves C back to place. C ver-
bally protests, "Not fair" etc all way back. Knocks door
shut on bench cupboard with knee – noticeable noise. Slams
bag down on bench – noticeable noise. Mr B stops talk,
fixes him with stare. C gazes back, eyes wide, mouth open.
Attentive, not hostile (innocent?). Mr B points at him,
arm out at full length. Severe warning issued – Mr B has
had enough this week from C. C will behave or else. No
exclusion this time; up to the Head. Last warning. Understand? C looks vaguely round. A & J enjoying this, smil-
ing, giggling, looking at each other and at C. He ignores
them (if he is aware of their approval, he gives no sign. No
eye contact, no smiles, no body language. This seems to be
only between him and Mr B.)*

There is no limit on the lengths of time over which recording takes
place. The observer's own time, determination, energy and concentration span will tend to be the limiting factors. Personal short-
hand and symbols can be devised to ease the strain of writing,
and detailed notes need only be taken when relevant events are
occurring. If C was quietly and attentively writing for 20 minutes,
that is all that needs to be recorded as far as the purpose of this
study is concerned. It is also usual for the observer's comments or
speculations, for example *(innocent?)* to be written in parenthesis.

By observing and documenting details of the events in the
pupil's day in this way, the researcher can build up a picture in
which patterns may be detected – for example, the interaction (or
lack of interaction) with peers, the shortening fuse of his teachers,
the kind of incidents which trigger disruptive behaviour. From
these patterns, mini-hypotheses can be generated and subsequently
tested by framing further questions to be addressed. Is disruptive
behaviour triggered when the child is ignored by a teacher? Does
the record show times when he was ignored and didn't disrupt?
Are there particular patterns of disruption linked to particular
teachers? What might be significant about the behaviour of these
teachers? And so on.

If the records are systematic and detailed, it may be possible
to extract quantitative data by designating categories, for exam-

ple, checking of behaviour, warnings, punishments, peer contacts etc and to quantify these in terms of their frequency of occurrence or duration in time.|These categories will not have been predetermined, however, but will have been perceived as patterns as the observations proceeded. The quantitative data would be used to support the qualitative descriptions,|for example: "C seldom experienced praise; over three days of continuous observation, he received three comments of praise about aspects of work and 89 negative comments: 74 about his behaviour and 15 about his performance".

[Narrative records can take a variety of forms. If as a researcher you are also a participant in the research context, retrospectively written records or diaries of your behaviour and experiences or those of others can form part of your data collection. Because the purpose of using this technique would be to understand complex social events, you would record broad segments of events over fairly lengthy periods of time in the same classroom, staffroom or school. You would be trying to get to know people and situations in order to understand them. You would be continually generating hypotheses from reading your written records, but you would regard these as tentative, to be confirmed, rejected or modified as further evidence arose from subsequent observations. |

Technological recording

Technological systems of recording comprise still photographs, videotape and audiotape. Some studies have used photographs or audiotapes to supplement other observational records, but video records could be regarded as full records on their own. With the advent of camcorders, video-making is now a relatively straightforward procedure even for non-professional filmmakers such as teachers and educational researchers.

However, you should give very careful consideration to the benefits which you feel this type of recording can bring to your study. Although at first sight recording on video or audio tape might seem like the best way to record observational data, on reflection you will see that it merely postpones the first stage of selecting and organising the data relevant to the investigation. Recording on video has some advantages, however. Although some choices must clearly be made concerning the events which are actually filmed, the video does offer a relatively 'unfiltered' record of all behaviours and transactions which occur in front of the camera and a permanent, detailed record is provided. The choices which are made – where to point the camera and how long to leave it running – constitute the sampling process and will be determined by the purpose of the study and the specific questions under consideration.

These factors will also determine how the video records are subsequently used. They may, for example, be run and re-run in order for a detailed systematic record, descriptive record, or narrative record to be made. Alternatively, they could be treated as narrative records, and a first level of analysis conducted on what is seen by running over the tape and noting or coding events as they occur. They can also be used as an aid to analysis in depth of what a teacher's perceptions or intentions were in a specific situation. It has been found that teachers will give a very rich and detailed account of what they were thinking, anticipating, intending etc if they are questioned in a non-threatening and open way (for example, 'Tell me, what was happening here?') about incidents and events which have just occurred in their classrooms or which are represented to them on video. This method of revealing the complexity of teachers' professional activities is much more effective than merely interviewing.

One of the disadvantages of video recording is its lack of flexibility when compared with the human observer/recorder. You may find that children get in the way of the camera, block out what is going on, or that key events 'off camera' are missed. Putting in two cameras to get round these problems simply doubles the amount of subsequent viewing and analysing time required and would almost certainly distort the natural events in the classroom which you had hoped to capture.

If your main interest is in observing your own practice, clearly video-recording is the only method you can employ. Many people who experience such viewing of their professional performance suffer a 'reality shock'. It may be that seeing yourself as others see you may be enough to give you significant pointers towards areas for change and development, without further analysis being necessary!

Although audio tapes can be treated as full records of oral transactions, many researchers have reported their inadequacy in this respect. In their study of young children, Tizard and Hughes (1984) had planned to use taped records of oral exchanges between children and adults as their basic data for analysis of interactions. They found many recordings inadequate or incomprehensible without additional information on the context of the interaction, including the associated non-verbal communications. Thus, while video records may sometimes be treated as full records, audio tapes are less useful unless accompanied by notes describing the context and other non-recorded factors associated with the oral exchanges, such as gestures, body posture, facial expressions, eye contact etc. However, they can provide a detailed record of oral interactions which may be vital for your study, if such detail is required to deal with your research questions.

Unfortunately, both video and audio tape recording take an inordinate amount of time to transform into transcripts. If you feel that recording by one of these methods is necessary for your study, do try a practice run first. It has been estimated that one hour of audio tape-recording can take up to 15 hours of a typist's and researcher's time for processing! For a few studies they can be an invaluable tool, for example in the detailed study of pupils' talk. If this is your area of interest, you may find Edwards and Westgate (1987) a useful and interesting source of information.

3
Managing the Activity of Observing

Once you are clear about the purpose of your study and you have refined the questions you want to answer, have decided on who and what you need to look at in order to get the answers, have more or less decided how to record your data and have surreptitiously practised your observation skills in the staffroom, the railway station and the supermarket, you will be ready to do your first serious, formal, practice run and to take the last few seemingly trivial decisions about the practical arrangements – such as 'Where do you stand?'

As soon as you start to plan your practice observations, you will become aware that questions such as 'Where do you stand?' – physically, professionally and ethically – are far from trivial, and need to be given serious consideration.

Where do you stand? – the physical setting

If you are observing in your own classroom you will be familiar with the setting. If you are observing in someone else's workplace it is useful to pay at least one preliminary visit and watch a 'typical' session of teaching and learning. This will help you to identify some of the practical problems you may encounter in conducting your formal observations. For example if you want to observe pupils, you have to decide where to sit. Too close, and you are likely to inhibit their natural activities, too far away, and you will miss a lot of what is going on. It is unfortunate for the observer that pupils in classrooms are now much more mobile than they used to be!

If you want to listen to pupil talk, you will need to be close enough to eavesdrop. But what if the target pupils move? Do you move around after them? How easy will this be? For example, does the teacher in a science class draw everyone round her at the bench half-way through the practicals? How do you follow a target individual or pair then? Planning data collection should be considered with regard to the actual setting. A practice run will help you determine how best to use your recording schedule, and what rules you adopt when recording does, and does not, take place. For example, you may decide that in looking at pupil-pupil talk you concentrate only on pupils as they work in pairs or groups, and omit the exchanges which occur in larger groupings. If you are using a tape recorder, where will you find convenient sockets? Every researcher knows the frustrating answer to that question!

The practice run will also help you identify other management problems. For example, you may find that events are occurring too rapidly for you to write down all you intended to record in freehand notes, or that you miss events because you are distracted by looking at your timer. You must find ways of dealing with these practical problems. For instance, if you are recording events at two-minute intervals, you can record a series of bleeps at two-minute intervals on a tape (both sides!) and be guided by this through an unobtrusive earpiece. If you find events happening too quickly for your note-taking, you could devise a code for frequently occurring events, for example:

TS SPQ –   The teacher scans round the classroom and selects a pupil to answer the question.

P NVol –   This pupil wasn't volunteering an answer.

Where do you stand? – roles and relationships

Whether you are observing pupils in your own classroom, pupils or colleagues in your own school, or teachers whom you have recruited as 'subjects' in a wider study, you need to give thought to your role and the relationships within the whole situation.

There is no doubt that observation is the most intrusive of all techniques for gathering data. People are quite happy to tick boxes in a questionnaire, and many may be pleased to voice their opinions on something if stopped in the street by a survey interviewer, although some may become nervous if you ask to tape or record their views. But if you ask if you can follow them around and watch and record, for future reporting, what they do for an hour or two each day or week, many people understandably become nervous and defensive and may find excuses to say 'no'.

Not only have you to be sensitive to those you are watching and build up a relationship of trust, you must be clear what your role is – the extent to which you are an objective, fly-on-the-wall observer, or a fully involved participant in the on-going events.

How to be a 'fly-on-the-wall'

If you are observing in someone else's classroom, it will be helpful if the teacher explains to the class that you are there simply to observe, not to participate in classroom activities. If you want to observe the classroom as it normally is when you are not present, you should be as unobtrusive as possible. Besides sitting where you can observe the relevant activities, try to sit where you will not obstruct or inhibit them. And you should signal, particularly to the pupils, what your role is. You can signal by your dress, or by how you talk with the pupils as you settle in and by what you are doing, that you are not another teacher in the classroom, and that they should not come to you for help. If you can avoid eye-contact with the children, you will send a clear signal that you are not prepared to be involved and will thus avoid any 'winding up' behaviour which is largely put on for your benefit.

If you are conducting observations in your own classroom, possibly while someone else takes your class, or while the pupils are doing some independent work, trying to adopt a 'fly-on-the-wall' role will have particular difficulties – both for you and for the pupils, who will still see you as their teacher. But the more you adopt this role and make it clear that you are, temporarily at least, opting out of your normal relationship with the pupils, the easier it will become for the new role to be accepted by both parties. Again, strategies such as avoiding eye-contact with pupils can help reinforce the message that something different is going on. The nature of your explanation to the pupils, and their interpretation of the implications will probably determine the extent to which they then behave 'normally' during your observation sessions.

Negotiating the ground rules

If your study requires that you observe in other people's class-rooms – possibly those of teachers who are strangers to you – there are a number of important factors to which you must give thought, and which should be communicated clearly to those who are recruited into your study.

- ## 'You have the right to refuse'

It is essential that those involved in your study are willing participants. However, there is a particular problem here for educational researchers. The educational system is hierarchical and it is therefore necessary that the interested parties at every level are involved in the decision-taking. If you are familiar with the local system and have friendly contacts at several levels, informal approaches are a useful way to begin sounding out what sort of reception your requests will receive. However, at an early stage, you *must* get permission to intrude officially into the school system and do it in such a way that all are reassured about your intentions. Some education authorities have guidelines and a specific person responsible for responding to requests for access to schools for research purposes. You must check whether this is the case in the local authority in which you intend to work.

These formal procedures are necessary for the protection of schools and cannot be avoided; nevertheless, they have one particular disadvantage you should try to deal with. If the authority asks the schools, the request may be seen as an imperative. 'We would like you to get involved in this research study but you don't have to say yes', may still sound like an invitation that can't be refused if it comes from an education authority to a headteacher or from a headteacher to one of the staff. Since such hierarchies will necessarily be involved in the selection of your schools or teachers, it is important for you to reassure those who have been selected of the voluntary nature of the involvement, and indeed to help them find an acceptable way of refusing, if they so wish.

And if the subjects of your observations are pupils in your own class or in someone else's classroom, do you have to ask their permission too – do they (or their parents) have the right to refuse to be included in your study? Some local authorities or schools have a policy on this too. In others, it will be a matter for your professional judgement based on consideration of the nature of the study and its context. You should think of the following:

- Is the study being undertaken by the normal staff of the school as part of their normal professional activities? Or will the observations of the pupils be undertaken by outsiders?

- Will the pupils simply be carrying on doing what they would normally be doing? Or will they be required to stop their normal classroom activities and engage in something different for periods of time?

- Is the purpose of this study to inform and improve the educational experiences of the pupils involved? Or are the observations part of a more formal or academic study of educational issues, for example, part of an MEd study, or of a regional or national research project?

- Is the study concerned with subject-oriented educational issues? Or does it concern sensitive areas such as guidance or social and personal education where personal or family issues might be exposed?

There are no hard and fast guidelines, but the nature of the study – the degree to which it deviates from normal school activities, involves outsiders, uses pupils as 'guinea pigs' or touches on sensitive issues – should be taken into account in deciding whether parents should be written to, asking permission for their child's involvement. If you have any reason to suppose that parents might need reassurance about what is going on in your own classroom, a letter simply explaining what the study is about might be sufficient to cover any possible future repercussions. However, local authorities, divisions and schools may have their own policies on this matter, and should be consulted.

- ### 'This is what will happen during the research'
You should explain to those you will be observing exactly what is involved and what they will be letting themselves in for – how often you want to be in their classroom, whether they can decide

when you can come, exactly what you want to watch, and why you have a particular interest in this aspect of their classroom. Fortunately, since classrooms and schools have become less formal, teachers are less uneasy about admitting others into their workplaces and it has also become easier for an observer to be unobtrusive – particularly in the hurly-burly of open-plan. If you are conducting a study in which pupils' learning in some area might need to be tested, or if you are setting up some situation, as a learning support teacher might do, looking at pupils performing a set task which you have devised, you must discuss the whole research programme with the teacher and negotiate about when, and indeed if, it would be possible to observe and test her pupils or set up your tasks in a corner of the classroom.

If you wish to observe some aspect of the teacher's behaviour, negotiations may become more delicate, but it would be quite unethical not to describe as fully as you can the areas of interest of your studies and perhaps to show them your observation schedule. Will this result in teachers behaving differently? Very possibly. But teachers are not exempt from the normal laws of human nature. Even the process of answering questions in an interview or questionnaire can make people reconsider their views on an issue with resultant changes in attitudes or behaviour.

• *'This is what will happen to the information'*

Most importantly, those who are being observed will need to be reassured about what will be done with all the information and notes about their activities or classroom which you have accumulated. They will want to know whether they can read them, whether you will change the records if they think you have misunderstood something, whether their headteacher will get to read the notes, and whether they will be identifiable in any published report, with their professional activities held up for general public scrutiny and comment as a consequence.

It is essential for you to think through, ahead of time, how you will respond to these concerns. Ideally you should give those involved something in writing which sets out the ground rules for your relationship which can be a focal point for discussion with those you wish to observe. A model of such a written 'contract' is given on page 88.

However, you will probably find that even a written contract may not allay all fears. Once the data collection is underway and you feel you are safely settled in the classroom or school and everything appears to be going well, it is not uncommon for a crisis to erupt, apparently, out of the blue. Teachers to whom you have initially explained your procedures and purposes will have accepted your statements and reassurances 'at face value'. A few weeks after the data collection has begun, they may find they want more detailed answers to questions that have subsequently occurred to them, been discussed in the staffroom and which have raised new doubts as to what is going on. It is essential to be sensitive to their growing awareness of what you are actually doing in their classrooms and the possible implications for them. It is essential to talk freely to them and their colleagues about your activities and to take seriously even apparently casual questions, for example, 'Who exactly is paying your expenses?' (ie Who are you working for? Who will you be reporting to?).

Where do you stand? – the ethical issues

As you will appreciate, observing others at close quarters as they go about their usual activities is the data-collection technique which intrudes most into people's 'personal space', and consequently may raise problems which tend not to occur when less intrusive techniques are used. In this section we present some examples of situations which researchers have encountered in the past and which you might experience in your own project.

Adopting coping strategies

Clearly, responses to events such as those we are about to discuss have the potential to distort data or to threaten the continuance of their collection. But there are no hard and fast rules to specify what you should do. The school or workplace in which you are observing is someone else's social territory and you are an intruder who must find ways of negotiating the terrain. You can give reassurances to others about your integrity and sound intentions and the confidentiality of the data, but you cannot force them to accept these. You can plan to adopt a stance of non-intervention, but your own feelings and values cannot be totally disengaged. You should use your professional knowledge, social skills and common sense to deal with whatever comes along. At the end of the day, it is your own conscience which should dictate what action you take.

Establishing your role

Although you may wish to present yourself in a school as the objective detached researcher, it is impossible to be a frequent visitor and to avoid becoming involved in the complex social life of a school. If you do not create a role for yourself, it may be created for you. You may be seen as a go-between for staff and management, as a spy whom management can choose to plant in suspect classrooms, as a lever for additional resources from the local authority, as a counsellor and confidante from outwith a closed and constraining community. With time and experience you will begin to recognise the signs that you are being asked to assume, or are being manoeuvred into, a role which is uncomfortable for you or improper for a researcher and you will need to signal clearly your own professional ground rules and role boundaries.

Reducing the level of 'threat'

Some participants may find the close scrutiny of an observer too intrusive for comfort, despite the reassurances given beforehand. Signs of annoyance towards you and hints, or indeed outright (false) accusations, that you are not keeping your side of the agreement, or are disrupting or impeding lessons, are signs that all is not going well and indicate that further reassurances and discussion about your activities and data collection are required. Remember that it may be much easier for you as an intruder to get settled into the observing situation than for the subject to feel comfortable with your scrutiny. You may find that, despite your best endeavours, some staff have indeed been coerced, or believe they have been coerced, into your study and that they never relax or appear to behave 'normally' while you are observing. If reassurances fail to ease the situation, you may have to consider dropping them from your study and seek replacements. The discomfort of being observed may also be reduced if the notes or records are shown to those involved. We have found that teachers are initially very curious to see what has been written about their classroom activities but, once they have read the records from our first few observations, they have been reassured enough to ask to be excused from the chore of reading any more!

Avoiding confrontation

You may find that despite the mutual acceptance of agreements on the confidentiality of data, a headteacher suddenly demands to see the notes from a particular classroom, or a teacher demands that you reveal what you observed some of her pupils were up to while she was busy elsewhere in the classroom. Such demands may be accompanied by the threat that, unless you concede their right to know what is going on, you will not be welcome back. Clearly it is desirable for all concerned that you try to resist, and reiterate your agreements about confidentiality, but if the threat is 'high stakes' – that is, you are liable to lose a significant amount of irreplaceable data – you could agree to discuss your data once you have cleared it with the persons observed; or you could share some general and uncontroversial points from your observations. If you have shared the records with the individuals concerned, as we have indicated above, their mystique is usually reduced. But how others will interpret and use your records is always outwith your control, and you should try to establish the principle of confidentiality at the beginning and ensure that it is mentioned frequently enough to be securely established as your study proceeds.

Turning a blind eye

You may find that, in the course of classroom observations of pupils, you learn of breaches of discipline, violations of school rules and even of criminal acts or intentions to commit criminal acts, for example the planning of a shoplifting expedition. You may find that, while you are trying hard to be a 'fly on the wall' and to observe and record objectively, some events are too painful merely to watch – for example, bullying or the persecution and victimisation of one child by others or, indeed, by a teacher. You may observe provocation which leads to violence between two children, with the victim subsequently being wrongly punished by the teacher. The extent to which observers can grit their teeth and not intervene, regarding such events as simply a shady corner of the rich tapestry of normal life, varies from individual to individual. There are no special rules for researchers in this area, and you should use the normal guidelines for professional discretion and consultation which are appropriate for the situation.

Where do you stand? – the claims you can make

If your research investigation goes beyond merely informing yourself about some feature of your classroom or professional life (as in Study 1 on page 4), and you wish to communicate your results to others, you will want to be sure that the data you have collected and the claims you are making stand up to public scrutiny.

Reliability and validity

Even modest claims can fail to stand up to scrutiny, unless they can be shown to be based on data which have two key characteristics – reliability and validity. How can you ensure, within your study, that your data are endowed with these two qualities?

Formal definitions of reliability can be found in every text on research methodology; however, with respect to the kind of data generated by observation, it is helpful to think of this term as referring to objectivity and dependability; that is to say, the extent to which any event would always be classified or described in the same way by the same person or by different observers.

If, for example, a number of teachers in your school decide to use the tally sheet on page 29 to compare data on how pupils behave in their classrooms, you need to take steps to make the categorisations of behaviour as objective and consistent as possible. Normally, this is done by getting different observers to look at the same events (for example, on a video), to categorise these events using the schedule, and then to compare the outcomes. You will probably find that some behavioural categories are easier to define and get agreement on than others, and so inter-observer agreement should be checked for each category. However, it doesn't matter if you can't come to agreement on some issues, as long as you agree that, *for the purposes of your study,* certain events will be classified in certain ways.

In a more formal study, you would wish to calculate the degree of inter-observer agreement for each category or variable, and the simplest way to do this is to calculate the percentage of observations in which two observers are agreed:

$$\text{percentage agreement} = \frac{\text{number of agreed observations}}{\text{total number of observations}} \times 100$$

A figure of lower than 80% would probably not be considered acceptable in a professional research study. A more sophisticated measure (the Scott coefficient) takes account of chance agreement by calculating how much better the observed level of agreement is than the level of agreement that would be generated by random processes (see Croll, 1986).

Within the less structured framework of qualitative data collection, how can reliability be enhanced? As we have already indicated, many decisions taken prior to the process of structured observation are postponed in qualitative research until the later stages, and therefore it is in the later stages that the reliability of the research data is enhanced. No research claims will stand up if they are based simply on impressionistic accounts of what someone saw. But clearly, the first stage is to go into the observation situation with as open a mind as possible, to avoid snap judgements and too early 'closure' on what the key issues are, and not to rule out consideration of alternative viewpoints and of data which do not fit with the argument you are developing.

During the course of a qualitative study, the sequence of observation sessions and the analysis of the data are conducted in parallel and the processes of data collection and processing should be geared towards making the data more reliable. This is achieved by making explicit the criteria for categorisation, and applying in a consistent manner the procedures for data selection, coding, grouping, inclusion, exclusion etc. The bases for these procedures should therefore be explicit and open to scrutiny and checking. Ideally, if someone else were to be given your data, along with an account of your procedures for data processing and descriptors of the constructs and categories which were applied, they should be able to replicate your data processing and come up with the same findings as you have done. These procedures are dealt with in greater detail in Chapter 4.

Having dealt with the soundness of your data collection, you then have to find solid ground on which to base your defence of its validity. This is a separate issue from reliability. You might have devised a schedule which yields the same data from several observers in the same classroom (that is, it is reliable), but whether it actually measures what you claim it measures – for example, teacher competence, effectiveness, civility, sanity, or whatever – may be hotly contested. How can you make your claim stand up? The strategy is to make your instruments, procedures and argument as *credible* as possible.

First, does it *seem* likely? This is called 'face-validity'. Observing children in the gym is unlikely to give you sound data about their emotional relationships and social values; observations conducted during Religious Education, Personal and Social Development, or Modern Studies, where 'caring for people' is being discussed, is a more credible source. Secondly, the claims that you make are more likely to stand up if you have evidence from a variety of sources to back them up; for example, additional questionnaire data from the pupils about their attitudes towards certain groups of people, scrutiny of written work from the pupils and interviews with them. The strategy of acquiring data on the same feature of interest from a variety of sources or perspectives is called 'triangulation' (see Cohen and Manion, 1994, Chapter 11). Thirdly, if a number of your colleagues agree, independently, that your schedule is appropriate for gathering the data you want, then your data collection is more likely to be valid. Another way of approaching this 'peer review' is to ask your colleagues to tell you what they think is the purpose of your schedule. This is a useful check on face validity, but depends on having access to colleagues who don't know what your intentions are before scrutinising your schedule.

What happens if you attend to all of these factors, but – at the reporting stage – those you have observed state flatly and forcefully that they simply do not recognise the account which your observations have yielded about their activities? Does this invalidate your study? Yes and no. Their disagreement does not mean that you are wrong and they are right, but suggests that in the course of your research you have omitted to take account of a valuable source of validating evidence – the views of the participants under observation. Entering into 'a free and open dialogue between observer and participant' is a key strategy for establishing validity. A leading researcher goes even further:

> 'And I would argue that it is only when an account has been agreed under these conditions of dialogue that its validity can be considered to be demonstrated. If agreement is not achieved under these conditions, then I would argue that a researcher's commitment to truth requires him to 'document the dialogue' in a way which clarifies the issues at stake.'
>
> Elliott (1990)

However, the key issue may be that different observers simply have different views of the world, and that these, while being irreconcilable, are equally valid.

> 'As observers and interpreters of the world, we are inextricably part of it: we cannot step outside our own experience to obtain some observer independent account of what we experience. Thus it is always possible for there to be different, equally valid accounts from different perspectives.'
>
> Maxwell (1992)

This is no justification, however, for slipshod research. You must justify your perspective by the presentation of reliable data, appropriate illustration and logical argument. If you would like to read more fully about the meaning and quality of evidence, you will find Anderson and Burns (1989), Chapter 6, very helpful.

Before going on to consider your data processing requirements, you perhaps need to stand back at this stage and review your research plan. Coming to a decision on your research questions (Chapter 1), your data collection procedures (Chapter 2) and your 'standing plan' (Chapter 3) is inevitably a cyclical process.

4

Processing Your Data

'The purpose of data analysis is to translate the evidence into a form which allows the researcher to make clear and concise statements of description and/or association.'

Anderson and Burns (1989, p 200)

Planning your analysis

When planning your research project you will have formulated specific questions and decided how to gather your data. In the early stages of your planning you should also have given thought to how you will actually process the data you plan to collect. Although the data analysis is normally undertaken at a late stage in the research enquiry, its planning is a crucial part of the early considerations given to the whole study. Giving thought to the processes of analysis will also help you to take sensible time-saving decisions about how to record the data. For example, many systematic observation schedules generate a lot of data and may require computer processing. It will save considerable time at the processing stage if the form of recording in the classroom can be used directly for data entry to the computer with only a checking procedure in between to ensure that no errors have crept in. Even if you don't eventually use a computer, it can still be very helpful to keep the amount of manual re-coding and sorting to a minimum. This not only saves time, it also reduces the number of stages at which errors might be made.

In Chapter 2 we described three ways of recording data – systematic, descriptive/narrative and technological. In this chapter we describe procedures for data analyses appropriate for the first two of these. Data recorded by technological systems are subsequently transformed to yield quantitative or qualitative information which can be dealt with by the data processing procedures we describe. It is also important to remember that there is no fundamental difference between the analysis of observational data – both quantitative and qualitative – and other types of research data. You will therefore find fuller description of many of the data analysis techniques in other texts, for example Turner and Clift, 1988, Chapter 3; Anderson and Burns, 1989, Chapter 7.

Analysing systematic records

The wealth of observational data which is normally collected allows for a great many data-analysis possibilities, from simple descriptions of individual categories to inter-relationships between multiple variables. However, care is needed in both the use of these data-analytic techniques and the interpretation of their results. For an exposition of cautionary measures and the more complex techniques you should consult Croll (1986). The use of a pre-constructed schedule to collect data suggests that you are clear in advance of undertaking your observations exactly what categories of variable you wish to investigate. The ways in which these data can best be processed should therefore also be clear. However, unexpected patterns may be suggested by the data. While discovering these unexpected patterns is part of the joy of doing research, it is often very frustrating, since, particularly with structured schedules, you will need to have built all the expected possibilities (ie categories of data) into your design. However, checking out the unexpected usually suggests that another study with a different design needs to be planned for the future. This is why even the most simple research almost always generates more questions than it answers!

Counting observations

Essentially there will be two dimensions to your systematic recording – the individual pupil, group of pupils, or teacher you are observing and the activities or behaviours in which you are interested. The very simple example of a tally sheet given on page 29 is focused on an individual pupil, John Smith, and his disruptive or learning-avoidance behaviours. These behaviours are not mutually exclusive – he can twist or clench his hands at the same time as he is making nonsense sounds. As long as every instance of these behaviours has been recorded there are various ways of analysing the data by simply totalling the tallies across time-intervals or subjects. You can then readily identify the pupil's most commonly displayed learning-avoidance behaviours, and also compare

- his pattern of behaviour in one class with that in another
- his patterns of behaviour at different times of the day, or days of the week
- his patterns of behaviour with those of other pupils who have also been observed at similar times and in similar contexts, using the same schedule.

In the second example of an event-driven recording system given on page 31, the teacher is the focus of observation, and three variables – relating to the teacher's questioning technique – are of interest.

Question type:	O: open	**Target pupils:**	B: boy	**Tone:**	J: jocular
	C: closed		G: girl		H: hectoring
			C: class		S: serious

Figure 4.1   Variables associated with teacher's questioning

Each of the variables associated with the teacher's questioning is characterised by two or three mutually exclusive and exhaustive categories (see Figure 4.1). For example, all the questions which are asked can be coded using the two categories 'closed' or 'open', and when a question is asked by the teacher, one category for each variable (question type, type of target and tone of question) must be selected for recording. In this case, another variable is also recorded and that is the time. By simply counting the various codes we can learn a lot about the particular teacher's pattern or style of questioning and, since there is a 'time line', we can also learn about patterns across time. As each question asked by the teacher is coded (the schedule is event-driven) the count gives us the frequency of different types of questions and so is best reported as a percentage or proportion, thus facilitating any comparisons we may wish to make – for example between different lessons or classes of the same teacher or between different teachers. Examples of the kinds of information which this type of schedule can give are given on page 32, and if a number of teachers have been observed, you can undertake comparisons.

Aggregating data

In the two examples discussed above, the basic unit of analysis is the event observation, but these data can be aggregated so that the pupil or the teacher who was observed can be treated as the unit of analysis.

It is a general rule that observational data collected on classes, individual pupils or events cannot be broken down later into 'smaller' units of analysis, but data can always be aggregated to serve different purposes, for example from events to pupils, or pupils to classes, depending on what we are trying to find out. An appropriate analogy here is that of 'fruit'. If you have gathered a number of things under the general category of fruit you cannot later find out how many apples and oranges there were. If you have gathered the data using the categories of apples and oranges, however, you can later lump them together as 'fruit'. You have to be careful, however, because both increasing the number of categories to get a finer grain view of events and the aggregation of data will lead to a consequent increase in the number of variables to be included. For example, if in using the schedule on page 31 the unit of analysis is the event (questioning by the teacher) then there will be three variables:

–   question type   (two categories)
–   target pupil(s)   (three categories)
–   tone of question   (three categories).

In this schedule the individual pupils are not identified; the research questions concern only gross categories of pupils – boys and girls. Any finer categorisation cannot be retrieved at the data processing stage. If you think a finer categorisation might yield more interesting and useful data, it *must* be built into the initial schedule. For example, 'bottom group boy' might be coded as B1; 'top group boy' as B2, etc. Increasing the fine grain of your pupil categories might then mean that your rate of recording needs to be adjusted in order to keep the schedule manageable. In other words, some hard decisions need to be made early on in the planning of the study as to the key variables which are of interest. But too much openness (that is to say, a large number of categories) built in at an early stage can lead to unmanageability, especially for inexperienced researchers.

If the data collected using the schedule are aggregated to the unit of analysis 'the teacher' then there will be eight variables, although they will not be independent of each other as those above:

number of open questions : number of closed questions
number of questions to boys : number of questions to girls :
number of questions to the class
number of x tone questions : number of y tone questions :
number of z tone questions

By treating the data in this way it is possible to compile in a relatively straightforward way descriptive comparisons between teachers of the type already indicated. More interesting would be cross-tabulations, for example the number of open questions directed at boys, to which we now turn.

Relationships between variables

Clearly, the more categories which are used, the more data points will be generated which must be dealt with. For example, if we used the DePICT-3 schedule, mentioned earlier, to collect 50 observations on each of 10 teachers we would have a 'file' of 500 cases (10 teachers x 50 observations) each having values for six variables. These data could be aggregated into a file of 10 cases (teachers) with 35 variables (all categories of the original six variables) each being a score of the number of occasions an observation was made in the category of the variable. The file of observations allows us to see associations between variables if particular categories occur together; the file of individual teachers allows us to see, not whether two things occur at the same time, but whether individuals with high values on one variable also tend to have high (or low) values on another.

For example, consider an observational study of three different classes. We are interested in any differences between the classes in terms of the seating arrangements of the pupils and their level of engagement with their tasks. We have chosen to observe five pupils in each of the three classrooms. The two variables under scrutiny are the pupils' seating arrangements:

- alone   A
- in pair   P
- in group   G
- in whole class C

and their degree of engagement in their task:

- distracted   D
- partially engaged   P E
- fully engrossed   F E

Observations are made using a time-driven system, that is, an observation is made concerning each pupil's seating arrangement and level of engagement every two minutes. The pupils are given identifying numbers (Pupil No) with pupils 1 to 5 coming from Class 1, pupils 6 to 10 from Class 2, and pupils 11 to 15 from Class 3. Each pupil is observed 20 times during each of two lessons giving 40 observations per pupil. The schedule for the two lessons observed for Class 1 would look something like Figure 4.2.

The data may subsequently be represented in a two-dimensional grid of 600 observations (15 pupils x 40 observations) x 2 variables (see Figure 4.3). The observations for each individual pupil have been grouped together in this grid; thus the observations are not now listed in the sequential order in which they were made.

Class 1	Observation No	Pupil No	Seating	Engagement
Lesson 1	1	1	A	D
	2	2	A	F E
	3	3	A	P E
	4	4	A	P E
	5	5	A	P E
	6	1	A	D
	7	2	A	F E
	8	3	A	P E
	9	4	P	D
	10	5	G	E
	11	1	A	D
	etc	–	–	–
	–	–	–	–
	–	–	–	–
	–	–	–	–
	–	–	–	–
	100	5	G	P E
Lesson 2	101	1	G	PE
	102	2	G	P E
	etc	–	–	–
	–	–	–	–
	196	1	A	F E
	197	2	G	P E
	198	3	A	P E
	199	4	G	F E
	200	5	G	P E

Figure 4.2 Schedule for engagement/seating observation record

Pupil No	Seating	Engagement	Class	Observation No
1	A	D	1	1
1	A	D	1	6
1	A	D	1	11
1	A	P E	1	16
1	A	P E	1	21
etc	–	–	–	–
–	–	–	–	–
1	A	F E	1	196
2	A	F E	1	2
2	A	F E	1	7
2	G	F E	1	12
2	G	F E	1	17
2	G	F E	1	22
etc	–	–	–	etc
–	–	–	–	–
5	G	P E	1	200

6	C	D	2	201
6	C	D	2	206
6	C	P E	2	211
6	C	P E	2	216
6	C	F E	2	221
etc	–	–	–	
–	–	–	–	–
10	G	D	2	400

11	C	D	3	401
etc	–	–	–	
–	–	–	–	–
15	A	F E	3	600

Figure 4.3   Grid for raw observation data

This grid preserves all the data and allows us to see at the same time what level of engagement is apparent with particular seating arrangements. Cross-tabulations of the data may be readily constructed which will show these patterns clearly. This would answer questions such as:

- What is an individual pupil's pattern of seating and engagement with task?
- Does s/he more commonly work alone and what level of engagement is there when working alone?

Figure 4.4 shows an example of a cross tabulation for one pupil.

		Level of Engagement			
		D	P E	F E	Total
Seating	A	3	10	2	15
Arrangement	P	5	5	0	10
	G	5	7	3	15
	C	0	0	0	0
	Total	13	22	5	40

Figure 4.4 Level of engagement and seating arrangement for one pupil

From this table we see that the pupil worked alone on 15 occasions, in pairs on 10 occasions, in groups on 15 occasions and in the whole class on none.

The pupil was distracted on 13 of these occasions, partially engaged on 22 and fully engrossed on 5 of them. When seated alone the pupil was most often partially engaged (10 occasions), when seated in pairs was distracted and partially engaged an equal number of times, and when in groups was most often partially engaged.

We can also construct cross tabulations for groups of pupils; in this example we are interested in comparisons between classes and so it is sensible to combine the data for each of the three groups of five pupils. For example:

		Level of Engagement			
Class 1		**D**	**P E**	**F E**	**Total**
Seating	A	5	55	10	70
Arrangement	P	25	15	10	50
	G	10	50	20	80
	C	0	0	0	0
	Total	40	120	40	200
Class 2		**D**	**P E**	**F E**	**Total**
Seating	A	5	15	30	50
Arrangement	P	0	0	0	0
	G	20	15	15	50
	C	25	50	25	100
	Total	50	80	70	200

Figure 4.5   Level of engagement and seating arrangement for pupils in two classes

From these two tables we see that, for example, pupils in Class 1 did not work as a whole class on any occasion in the two lessons observed and that pupils in Class 2 did not work in pairs. The predominant seating arrangement in Class 2 was as a whole class and the seating arrangement in which pupils were fully engrossed most often (proportionately) was alone. Many more statements of this nature may, of course, be made.

For many research questions we may want to work with the data for each pupil, rather than for each observation. For example, combining the observation data for each pupil shows how individual pupils differ in both their seating arrangements and levels of engagement and pupils may be compared on these two variables in order to answer questions such as: Does pupil X have a different pattern of seating arrangement from pupils Y and Z? Which pupil is most often distracted?

The combined data for each pupil may be represented in another grid (15 pupils x 7 categories, now variables).

	Variables							
	Seating Alone	Seating in Pairs	Seating in Group	Seating in Class	Engagement Distracted	Engagement Partial	Engagement Full	C
Pupil 1	20	10	10	0	10	20	10	
Pupil 2	20	0	20	0	0	30	10	
–	–	–	–	–	–	–	–	
–	–	–	–	–	–	–	–	
–	–	–	–	–	–	–	–	
–	–	–	–	–	–	–	–	
Pupil 15	10	0	10	20	10	10	20	

Figure 4.6 Level of engagement and seating arrangements for individual pupils

The categories of the two original variables A, P, G and C in seating arrangement, and D, PE, FE in degree of engagement, may now be regarded as variables and the number of instances of each counted for each pupil, for example, the number of times a pupil is seated alone, or is distracted. What has been lost in this aggregation of data to the level of pupil is the direct link between seating arrangement and level of engagement. We can see that pupil 1 was most often seated alone and most often partially engaged. We don't know if this partial engagement occurred when seated alone, or in pairs, or in groups. Clearly, the variables formed from the categories of variables in the raw data are not independent – pupils who have a high 'score' on being distracted cannot also have high scores on partial and full engagement.

What has been gained in this aggregation of data is the facility to employ statistical techniques, for example to describe individual variables through means and standard deviations (best expressed as proportions or percentages), and to explore interrelationships between variables through correlations of independently derived variables or comparisons of means. Average values of variables can also be compared for different groups (for example, boys, girls, different subject lessons, classes). For a more detailed account of the processing of quantitative data from observation schedules, see Croll (1986).

Analysing descriptive and narrative records

In dealing with the analysis of qualitative data, as with the analysis of data from systematic recording (quantitative data), the appropriate analytic techniques are not necessarily particular to information collected from observation, but apply also to data collected by other means, for example, by interview.

The major difference between using pre-structured schedules to gather data (the researcher using an instrument) and strategies for unstructured qualitative data collection (the researcher as an instrument), is the timing of the decisions about what it is important to observe and to focus on in analysis. The researcher using a structured instrument has made these decisions before beginning the observations and once all the observations have been completed, data analysis begins. The researcher acting as the instrument through the writing of field notes makes the decisions at the time the events occur and in the course of data processing. The subsequent observations and data analysis serve to focus, refine, verify, organise, reduce and present the data. The investigative process is thus a cyclical one of data collection and processing – observing, recording, reading, reflecting, coding, further data collecting, re-reading, reflecting, re-coding ... etc, in order to make gradual sense of complex social phenomena. The rigour applied to qualitative data collection and analysis is thus no less than that applied to quantitative procedures. As theories about the meaning of events are generated, data which support or challenge these theories must be sought.

For example, if the extract on page 49 was written at a very early stage in the study, reading the account might prompt a number of questions which the researcher would keep in mind during coding and subsequent observations, and which would serve to confirm or refute the possibility that some of the factors identified (for example, roles of peers) were important. For instance, in reading over the notes taken during the first observation, the following questions might be raised:

- Does C ever involve other pupils, or is he always apparently detached from engagement with them?
- Does C confront some teachers more than others?
- What are the key characteristics of these different teachers?
- Are teachers consistent in the ways they typically respond to him – and does he vary his behaviour to correspond to differences between teachers?

And so on. These questions are still tentative and exploratory, but they are beginning to make more explicit the interpretive frameworks which might begin to structure the research. Discussions with others at this stage are extremely useful. They can help the researcher avoid the pitfalls of relying too much on the ideas which they themselves bring to the interpretation, rather than letting the data 'speak to them', and of foreclosing too quickly on alternative ways of construing and interpreting what is being observed.

If the account on page 49 was written very late in the study, it is likely that the key elements of interest and significance would be well established and the key categories in the whole episode might be fairly quickly coded.

How do you know what to code? The key aim in processing qualitative accounts is to organise the data into categories representing characteristics, patterns or themes, and then to illustrate and provide supportive evidence and arguments for these as valid interpretations of what has been observed.

The analysis of the data should thus generate explanations as defensible accounts of the situation being investigated. This is done by searching the data, generating categories which account for the data, and which allow interpretation, providing evidence for these interpretations, and repeatedly reviewing the data, seeking both confirmatory and contradictory evidence. The latter is particularly important. You may need to revise the assertions as the analysis proceeds; all the information which contradicts your interpretations – the discrepant cases – needs to be analysed, and may well offer deeper insights into your original assertions. Repeated readings of the observation records are the starting point – using coloured pens, cutting and pasting on to file cards (you will need multiple copies of the records for this) or a set of codes to highlight evidence for or against the major assertions. The categories you develop should be exhaustive – able to deal with all your data, and mutually exclusive – they should not be overlapping so that data could fit in more than one category; and the decision-taking process of allocating data to one category or another should be based on simple criteria.

For example, in the initial stages, the episode with Mr B might generate detailed, descriptive, simple coding:

C   – a confrontational episode
M   – male teacher
ET   – empty threats issued
NP   – no interaction with peers
4B   – the fourth episode in a series of linked interactions
        with Mr B
     – etc

These codes could initially be marked on the text with coloured pens. After reading and re-reading a number of accounts and undertaking further observations, the researcher might decide that pupil C's interactions with teachers have features which allow them to be classified under three general headings: confrontation (C), soliciting nurturance (SN), and performing to please (PP). A table showing the incidence of these with respect to other features, such as the gender of the teacher, or the kind of rules which the teacher imposes, would perhaps allow other patterns and relationships to be seen.

Quite often, odd patterns emerge and you have to think, 'What is this an instance of? Is there a set of different categories or a higher order pattern here?' Reading the literature dealing with similar research studies and discussing with colleagues can prove immensely helpful. For example, much work has been done on 'classroom norms' – a shared or imposed set of standards considered appropriate and essential for good functioning in the classroom. There may be a number of 'norms' which C challenges – the 'quietness norm', the 'deference norm' etc; and this may interact with 'deviance latitude' – the extent to which different teachers allow deviance from his/her norms – a degree of latitude which is negotiated by a particular class or by individuals through the establishment of good relationships, or by the use of trade-offs, or coercion etc. It may well be that hitherto inexplicable behaviour on the part of C can be interpreted and understood in terms of these concepts, and your argument that this is so can be supported and illustrated by your data.

Having got to this level of analysis, the researcher might then wish to go back and re-read some accounts coded earlier, and reconsider the coding. Computer software packages are now available to aid this process (see, for example, Fielding and Lee, 1991) but this does not replace the need for the researcher to read and re-read the text, drawing out both recurrent patterns and instances which run contrary to those patterns, to seek out alternative explanations, to rule out spurious relationships between data, and to use cases which show deviances from the others, or which show extreme forms of key characteristics, as a basis for further exploration and interpretation.

Ultimately you may be testing out the theoretical interpretations of others, for example concerning the 'norms' of the classroom and their characteristics, or you may be generating new ideas for further development and testing. As we have already shown (see page 51), information gathered in a qualitative form can also be used to generate quantitative data, but it is likely to be of a descriptive nature only – such as percentages – and could not appropriately be subjected to statistical analysis. Delamont (1992) and Miles and Huberman (1984) give lengthy accounts of the specific strategies and processes involved in analysing qualitative data, and the interested reader is referred to these for more detailed descriptions of the methods.

However, here are some fairly basic general rules:

- Don't let piles of unattended data accumulate

  – set time aside to read over your notes and begin your coding.

- Start by coding *densely*, ie code a large number of things

  – don't start summarising too quickly, and don't worry about having too many codes; things will start to come together as you go along.

- Stop and think; read around the literature

  – the data will speak to you, but you should give time and thought to understanding the messages, and they may not always confirm what you wanted to hear!

- Keep track – don't get lost in the data processing

  – get a good system for handling the paperwork and keeping track of key things – of who you watched, the main codes, what the definitions of the categories were, the thoughts which occurred to you, the questions you decided to pursue (and why), the questions you decided not to pursue (and why not).

- 'Trust your intuitions – but don't fall in love with them.'

  (Miles and Huberman, 1984)

  – respond to what you think is plausible when you generate your categories and interpretations – but remember, you might be wrong! Verify your data and your ideas by testing them out, through further observations, with those observed, against all your data, and with documentary evidence from other sources.

There are a number of commonly-used specific techniques:

Counting: when we identify a theme or pattern, we isolate something that (a) happens a number of times and (b) consistently happens in a specific way. If something 'seems' to be said or done by a lot of people – check it out by counting.

Noting patterns, themes: something jumps out at you – and you see a pattern. That part is easy – but it needs to be checked out, tested, demonstrated to be sound.

Clustering: what things go together, which do not? This is part of the process of moving to higher levels of abstraction. Things might go together because they fulfil the same function (see page 33), or because they share certain key attributes etc.

Making metaphors: metaphors can be marvellously useful for capturing the essence of something and communicating it in a vivid way to others, without the dryness associated with much research reporting. For example, 'Some pupils were grit in the well-oiled machine of his complex maths scheme'. But do not look for metaphors too early. They are data-reducing, and can distract you from taking a more detailed analytical look at what is actually there.

Splitting variables: generally you will be trying to integrate categories, to find higher-order descriptions. But sometimes you will need to dis-integrate. For example, different types of encounters may be classed as 'confrontational' before it becomes clear that there may be different kinds of confrontations, and that relationships between these episodes and other variables become clearer when this single category is broken down into several distinct sub-categories.

Subsuming particulars into the general: once you have gone through your initial simple coding, you will move towards clustering, for example, a number of different activities could be described as 'keeping the classroom clean'. The next stage is the generation of more abstract categories, for example, 'the cleanliness norm'. These abstract categories are not arbitrary, they will have to relate to the key questions you are trying to address and will move your interpretation and thinking forward.

Making conceptual/theoretical coherence: the last stage is finding whether there are some general theories or constructs which contribute even further to the understanding of the data and hence the events from which they are derived. This is when reading the literature can help – there may be theories in social psychology, anthropology, child development etc which will allow you to set your findings in a more general framework and allow a deeper understanding and wider communication of your findings. |

In Conclusion

We have now, as authors, come to that point which, in the process of doing a research project, is always the most difficult – that of finishing. It is a universally acknowledged feature of doing research that the data collected will never answer all the questions which are raised in your study, and it will always seem that just one more set of observations, a few more interviews, or one or two visits to another school are all that are needed to get it rounded off or complete. It seldom happens that way. You will simply open up more territory which invites exploration. 'Life proliferates endlessly', observed Miles and Huberman (1984), and if you don't put sharp boundaries down in terms of the time spent, the volume of data collected and the energy expended, the research can take over your life. The collection of data must be stopped, the data processing must be completed and the findings must be communicated.

As Delamont (1992) said, 'Don't get it right, get it written!'

Further Reading

Delamont, S (1992) *Fieldwork in Educational Settings, Methods, Pitfalls and Perspectives*. Falmer.

For some, research is not merely a professional activity, it is a way of life and the motivating force is 'lust of knowing what should not be known'. This book, 'cheerful and optimistic' and written by a leading qualitative researcher, gives a lively and illuminating account of the joys and despairs, the challenges and delights of travelling across uncharted territory and retrieving treasures of great worth through the application of the observation and data collection skills of the determined field worker.

Anderson, L W & **Burns, R B** (1989) *Research in Classrooms: the Study of Teachers, Teaching and Instruction*. Pergamon.

Two chapters in this book, Chapter 6 'The Meaning and Quality of the Evidence', and Chapter 7 'Issues in the Analysis of Evidence', provide valuable information on a range of factors which are important in the collection and processing of data from observational investigations.

Cavendish, S, Carlton, M, Hargreaves, L & **Harlen, W** (1990) *Observing Activities*. Chapman.

In three sections of this paperback book you will find useful, practical information on using observation schedules in classrooms: Section 3, 'Observing the Classroom Systematically'; Section 4, 'The Science Process Observation Categories'; Section 6, 'Observation by Teachers'.

Croll, P (1986) *Systematic Classroom Observation*. Falmer.

This is the most detailed text dealing with all aspects of the use of systematic observation schedules.

Evertson, C M *&* **Green, J L** (1986) *Observation as Inquiry and Method.* In: **Wittrock, M C** (ed) *Handbook of Research on Teaching.* Macmillan.

If you wish to read a fairly academic account of the theory and practice of observing as a research data collection technique, this article should be of interest.

Dunkin, M (ed) (1987) *The International Encyclopaedia of Teaching and Teacher Education.* Pergamon.

In a series of articles in this text book, leading writers in key fields present condensed, but very accessible and readable, accounts of aspects of research theory and practice. For example: *Structured Observation* (M Galton); *Naturalistic Inquiry* (E G Guba and Y S Lincoln); *Ethnographic Methods* (R Taft); *Units of Analysis* (L Burstein).

Sanger, J (1994) Seven Types of Creativity: looking for insights in data analysis. *British Educational Research Journal*, 20 (2) 175-185.

Adopting 'a position of anarchic disenchantment with the rigidity and conservatism which constrain research activity' this author presents a personal view of alternative approaches to data analysis which will either fire you with renewed enthusiasm or drive you to exasperation and despair – it all depends on where you are standing and, of course, how you choose to interpret what you see!

A Sample Contract

1 Individual staff in the school will be in agreement to participate in the project. In the case of any pupils who are to be studied intensively or over a long period, parental consent will be necessary.

2 School staff will indicate to the researchers the time which they are willing or able to allocate to interview etc.

3 The information given by any interviewee and any observation notes taken in any classroom will be confidential to the teacher involved and to the immediate College research team. All data collected from individual pupils will be treated with similar respect.

4 The transcripts of any interviews with teachers and observation notes on their activities will be made available to the teacher involved if requested, for comment and amendments. Any changes requested will be made.

5 Discussions with the pupils about their work will take place in classrooms only following prior consultation and agreement with the teacher.

6 Data will be extracted from the interviews and observations and used to illustrate 'main points' in the final report. Where direct quotes are used, no individual will be named or otherwise identified.

7 Should it be agreed with a teacher that the compilation of a full case study of a particular classroom or child is considered valuable for dissemination, it will be necessary for all the participants concerned in that part of the study to give their permission for the data to be presented in this way, and to agree on the final presentation.

References

Anderson, L W (1984) Concerns for appropriate instrumentation in research on class-room teaching, *Evaluation in Education: an International Review Series,* 8, 113-152.

Anderson, L W & Burns, R B (1989) *Research in Classrooms: the study of teachers, teaching and instruction*. Pergamon Press.

Burstein, L (1987) Units of analysis. In: **Dunkin M J** (ed) *The International Encyclopaedia of Teaching and Teacher Education*. Pergamon.

Cavendish, S, Galton, M, Hargreaves, L & Harlen, W (1990) *Observing Activities*. Chapman.

Cohen, L & Manion, L (1994, 4th edition) *Research Methods in Education*. Routledge.

Corsaro, W A (1981) Entering the child's world: research strategies for field entry and data collection in a pre-school setting. In: **Green, J L & Wallat, C** (eds) *Ethnography and Language in Educational Settings*. Ablex Publishing.

Croll, P (1986) *Systematic Classroom Observation*. Falmer.

Delamont, S (1992) *Fieldwork in Educational Settings: methods, pitfalls and perspectives*. Falmer.

Edwards, A & Westgate, D (1987) *Investigating Classroom Talk*. Falmer.

Elliott, J (1990) Validating case studies, *Westminster Studies in Education* 13, 47-60.

Fielding, N G & Lee, R M (eds) *Using Computers in Qualitative Research*. Sage.

Galton, M & Patrick, H (eds) (1990) *Curriculum Provision in the Small Primary School*. Routledge.

Galton, M, Simon, B & **Croll, P** (1980) *Inside the Primary Classroom.* Routledge and Kegan Paul.

Goffman, E (1961) *Asylums: essays on the social situation of mental patients and other inmates.* Penguin.

Hargreaves, L (1990) Teachers and pupils in small schools. *In:* **Galton, M** & **Patrick, H** (eds) *Curriculum Provision in the Small Primary School.* Routledge.

McAlpine A, Brown S, McIntyre D, & **Hagger H** (1988) *Student Teachers Learning from Experienced Teachers.* The Scottish Council for Research in Education.

McCail, G (1991) *Pre-five Environment Quality Rating Scale.* Moray House Institute of Education, Heriot-Watt University.

Maxwell, J A (1992) Understanding validity in qualitative research, *Harvard Educational Review*, 62, 279-300.

Miles, M B & **Huberman, A M** (1984) *Qualitative Data Analysis.* SAGE.

Morris, D (1977) *Manwatching: a field guide to human behaviour.* Cape.

Pollard, A (1985) Opportunities and difficulties of a teacher-ethnographer. In: **Burgess, R G** (ed) *Field Methods in the Study of Education.* Falmer.

Powell, J (1985) *The Teacher's Craft.* The Scottish Council for Research in Education.

Simpson, M, Cameron, P, Goulder, J, MacPherson, A, Duncan, A, Roberts, A, Smithers, I (1989) *Differentiation in the Primary School: investigations of learning and teaching.* Northern College of Education.

Tizard, B & **Hughes, M** (1984) *Young Children Learning.* Fontana.

Turner, G & **Clift, P** (1988) *Studies in Teacher Appraisal.* Falmer.

Weldon, F (1976) *Remember Me.* Hodder and Stoughton, Coronet edition, 1979, pp22–24.

Woods, P (1986) *Inside Schools: ethnography in educational research.* Routledge & Kegan Paul.